THIS

journal

BELONGS TO:

....

ALSO BY KRISTEN BUTLER

*The Comfort Zone: Create a Life You Really
Love with Less Stress and More Flow*

*3 Minute Positivity Journal: Boost Your Mood.
Train Your Mind. Change Your Life.*

All of the above are available at your local bookstore,
or may be ordered by visiting:

Hay House USA: www.hayhouse.com®

Hay House Australia: www.hayhouse.com.au

Hay House UK: www.hayhouse.co.uk

Hay House India: www.hayhouse.co.in

3 MINUTE

happiness

JOURNAL

SUSTAINABLE FORESTRY INITIATIVE
Certified Chain of Custody
Promoting Sustainable Forestry
www.sfiprogram.org
SFI-01268
SFI label applies to the text stock

CREATE HAPPY HABITS. CHANGE YOUR BRAIN.
TRANSFORM YOUR LIFE.

3 MINUTE
happiness
JOURNAL

KRISTEN BUTLER

FOUNDER OF **POWER OF POSITIVITY**

Contents

Don't forget, while you're busy doubting yourself, someone else is admiring your strength.

@POSITIVEKRISTEN

Introduction

Welcome! Hello, I'm Kristen.

I am so excited to be on this happiness journey with you. Congratulations on deciding to uplevel your mindset with me and move your life forward in a happier, more fulfilled direction.

We're going to be taking small, subtle steps each day, but it's going to equal huge happiness and reliable results by the end. The next few months are going to be epic! Possibly even life-transforming!

When I started sharing positive quotes and affirmations with the Power of Positivity community on Facebook in 2009, I had no way of knowing that someday this page would attract millions of people from across the globe, and that the PoP brand would grow into a community of over 50 million across multiple platforms.

Just a few short years before, all I wanted was relief from my own internal pain, anxiety, and self-deprecating thoughts that had led me to live with extreme stress and eventually culminated in depression, overwhelm, and burnout.

I remember looking at myself in the mirror and being disappointed by my own reflection. I had spent over two weeks in bed, feeling sorry for myself and entertaining the idea that it might be better if I just didn't exist. I felt unworthy, unlovable, unhappy, and incapable of doing anything worthwhile.

Over the course of the previous year, I had seen all my dreams fall apart, one by one. My business was in bankruptcy, my body was obese, my mind was filled with doubt and self-judgment, and I was carrying unhealed trauma. The last straw was my physical health; it was so poor that doctors told me I would never have children. I felt like I had failed my life purpose, my family, and God.

I had nothing to live for, nothing to be excited about, no way out of the deep dark hole I had dug for myself. I felt so stuck that I hated my life. It was during one particularly dark night that I reached a pivotal moment. I realized that I had a decision to make. I felt I was too young to give up, but I could not bear living the way I had been living. I needed a drastic change—a new path. I prayed. I asked for strength to pull through. Sobbing, I asked for a sign. "Please, point me in the right direction."

The next day, I saw a meme with a positive quote on it. A few days earlier, I would have dismissed the quote, rejecting the idea that a positive mental attitude might make a difference. But that day, it struck a chord deep within me. It made me feel seen and understood. That's when I knew.

I had to start accepting the person in the mirror, flaws and all.

It was time to stop living for approval and other people's expectations and needs. I had to focus on myself and fill my own cup if I wanted true happiness. I couldn't take action or succumb to inaction from a place of not-enough-ness. I had to begin with learning to love myself—all of myself.

For the first time in years, I asked myself what I needed. Not what I needed to do for other people. Not what I needed to accomplish. Not what I needed others to think about me.

No. I asked, "Kristen, right now, in this moment, what do you need?"

The answers started to come to me slowly but with clarity.

"I need to take a long bath."

"I need to walk around the block."

"I need to read something uplifting."

The small actions I took started to pull me out of rock bottom. I finally felt relief from the judgment I had projected onto myself, and as I did, I started feeling more comfortable in my body, more confident with my choices. These small acts started to form a morning routine that allowed me to start my day feeling better than I had in years. I began calling these my "happiness habits" because when I did them consistently, I felt happier, more alive, more loving, and more in control of my daily experiences.

Each day, I became more consistent with my happiness habits and the results started to show in every single area of my life. Deeply rooted thought patterns started to shift in my subconscious as I loved myself and cared for my own needs. False belief systems about always putting others first started to fade away. Beautiful thoughts about who I was, why I was here, and how I could contribute to this world

started to take root. Defeating thoughts about my current situation started to be replaced with hope and faith that things would get better.

That's when I realized: taking care of yourself is not selfish, it's the key to happiness. Making your own happiness a top priority allows you to care for those around you more deeply.

That's why I created this journal for you! I want you to experience true, lasting happiness that comes from within you. I want you to be happy, even amid challenges. I want you to feel grateful for the journey you are on. The guidance, prompts, and activities in this journal are intentionally created by me for YOU. They are a culmination of over a decade of research, learning, observation, exploration, and experimentation. These concepts are also backed by science—which I love! I've used these to transform my life and I want you to do the same. And when your life transforms in the most beautiful and magical ways, I want to hear your success stories. I want you to shine!

Why Is Happiness Important?

I know you want to be a happier person or you wouldn't be here reading these words. But setting a goal to live a happy life is not something that just magically happens; you must intentionally create it. Happiness takes commitment and practice.

Optimism is a skill. It's not magic, although over time it can create results that feel magical. It's important to prioritize your happiness because it creates healthy self-esteem and self-love. Researchers[1] studying healthy self-esteem say that self-love helps to promote positive mental health and well-being. What a beautiful, positive feedback loop! When you show up for yourself and your own happiness, you, in turn, boost how you feel about yourself and your life.

SCIENCE SAYS HAPPINESS HELPS YOU LIVE HEALTHIER AND LONGER

Science agrees that happiness is important, and even seeking happiness can make you happier! In recent years, many studies have analyzed the impact of our emotions on our health and quality of life. These studies have shown that happier people feel a greater sense of purpose and well-being, solve problems better, and surround themselves with more positive people.

Studies also show that happy people don't just enjoy life more, they also live longer. When you feel good and you are genuinely happy in your own skin, it positively affects your health, your mood, and your relationship with everyone else around you. You lower your risk of cardiovascular disease, you lower your blood pressure, you sleep better, eat better, and boost your immune system. If that isn't enough motivation for you to prioritize happiness, after two decades of research, the HeartMath Institute discovered that your attitude can literally alter your DNA, allowing you to renew your body and mind on a cellular level and protecting you against illness.[2]

Sometimes I need to go off on my own. I'm not sad. I'm not angry. I'm recharging my batteries.

@POSITIVEKRISTEN

A happy disposition has an unparalleled effect on your life—one I've experienced firsthand. The happier I have become, the healthier and more fulfilled I feel. The more I've prioritized feeling good, the more things I have attracted into my experience that feel good and fulfilling for me. I've come to realize that when I'm not feeling good, it's because I am neglecting my own needs and not prioritizing joy. When I make an intentional effort to improve my mood, I always feel more like myself and better in my body.

HAPPINESS IS AN INSIDE JOB—DON'T ASSIGN IT TO OTHERS

In this journal, my goal is to share with you all my own happiness habits so that you can start feeling better every day, and as you do, you can start cultivating a life that feels fulfilling.

My dream for you is that the happiness habits in this journal become a part of your self-care routine and that you use them as a launching pad to shift your energy every day into a happier place, so that you can take advantage of the myriad benefits that a joyful, positive disposition provides.

Optimism is the key to inner happiness.

Your circumstances do not create a positive attitude; you must feel good about where you are to be happy—no matter your circumstances. This journal will help you discover this truth. I hope that the consistency of using this happiness journal daily for the next 90 days helps you establish a lasting routine in your own life and that it helps you create and start believing and pursuing your dreams.

Before we dive into the journal entries, I want to talk briefly about emotions.

You are a thinking and feeling being. This is wonderful, because your emotions, whether they are positive or negative, allow you to experience the richness of life.

When I was feeling depressed and depleted, it was hard for me to accept that even my negative emotions are a gift, because they allow me to experience the full range of the human experience. I naturally wanted to stop suffering, even to the point that I felt my only way out of my pain was ceasing to exist.

As I started to do the things that made me feel better, I realized that there was an incredible amount of information and wisdom in my pain. My negative emotions were not there to make me suffer; they were guides. They were showing me that I had gone down a path that was in conflict with my true desires and needs. As I started to pay attention to my needs and prioritize doing the things that filled my cup, I naturally started to feel better.

Too often, we give away our own power by making other people, events, and circumstances responsible for our emotions. We say things like:

"He makes me so angry."

"She's the reason I'm depressed."

"I'm too stressed because nothing ever works out for me."

It's natural to do this. In the past, I also used other people, events, and circumstances to justify my emotions, especially if I was feeling terrible. But as long as someone or something else was responsible for my pain, I had no power. I was a victim. And as long as I was a victim, I had no way out of the darkness.

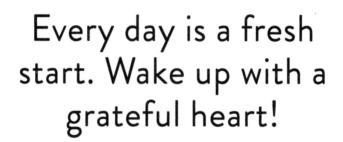

Every day is a fresh
start. Wake up with a
grateful heart!

@POSITIVEKRISTEN

The most transformative moment in my life was when I decided to take responsibility for my own emotional state. When I stopped blaming others or making excuses for myself. When I said, "Kristen, you got yourself into this mess. You can get yourself out of it."

When you take responsibility for your emotions—both positive and negative—you finally take charge of your life.

Becoming aware of your emotions is an important step toward no longer being at the mercy of them.

In her best-selling book *My Stroke of Insight*, Dr. Jill Bolte Taylor states that the natural life cycle of an emotion is just 90 seconds. This means that if you don't "hook into" the emotion with your explanations, justifications, and storytelling, the physical sensation of the emotion will leave your system within 90 seconds. When an emotion lingers beyond this point, you have chosen to keep it active.

As you go through the exercises in this journal, I hope you will take this to heart and take full responsibility for how you feel. When you feel negative emotions, instead of explaining, justifying, or blaming, I hope you'll say something like, "I feel frustrated right now, but I know I can feel better. What are some things I can do or think right now that can help me feel better about this situation?" In this way, you identify and release the negative emotions and begin to create positive ones.

If you can do this, you'll shorten your path from every emotion to happiness. You'll also realize that your happiness, joy, fulfillment, and purpose do not depend on anyone else. The happiness you discover within yourself is always present and always available to you. Once you learn to access it, you'll be able to tap into it anytime you desire.

GRATITUDE IS THE BEST ATTITUDE

This journal is about creating happy habits so you can start making your own happiness a priority. This is how you replenish your own reserves so you can continue to give back to those you love without feeling depleted. Acknowledging the silver linings and finding things to be grateful for every single day is an important part of this journey and is a practice you'll be participating in daily—both morning and evening—within the pages of this book.

Gratitude is perhaps one of the most underrated yet most transformative tools you have to live a life full of happiness. Gratitude will not only shift your energy and rewire your brain, it will turn you into a magnet for everything that you appreciate. To find true, lasting happiness that is rooted deep within you, you must cultivate an attitude of gratitude.

If your happiness is yours and comes from within you, no one can ever take it away.

The happier you are, the more you appreciate your life, and the more you attract to yourself people, experiences, and things that bring you joy.

That's why I believe journaling is the perfect way to shift your emotions immediately and process your feelings without judgment, so you don't get stuck in unpleasant experiences. All you need to do is show up and do the exercises in this journal, and you'll become the driver of your own vehicle of life experiences instead of letting life take over and drive your days.

The goal is to create and nurture a thriving internal environment of happiness that you can take with you wherever you go.

When you put effort in these pages day by day—morning and evening—something starts to shift inside and you slowly begin to align yourself with who you want to be, where you want to go, and how you want to feel. If you have already completed the *3 Minute Positivity Journal*, then you have already witnessed this truth. If you haven't, you're in for a wonderful treat. Over time, people in your life will notice a change in you and will ask what you are doing differently.

LET'S STAY CONNECTED ON THIS JOURNEY!

I am so excited for you to get started! Whether you are going through a tough time right now or you just need a little extra boost of inspiration and accountability, please know that we are in this together. I want to invite you to connect with me on social media. You can find me on Instagram and other social media platforms with the handle @positivekristen. I look forward to hearing about your journey over the next 90 days. Shine on!

Text "Happiness" to 828-237-6082 for more inspiration.

Currently only available to the USA and Canada.

Power of POSITIVITY

25 Morning Happiness Habits

A morning routine is pivotal in keeping your mood elevated throughout the day. Here are some morning happiness habits that I personally love that will help you wake up in a good mood, keep the happy vibes flowing, and have an amazing day!

- prayer
- gratitude
- journaling
- 30 minutes of no tech
- watching the sunrise
- mindful tea or coffee
- making your bed
- exercise
- visualization
- meditation
- reading
- healthy breakfast
- going for a walk
- drinking water
- writing
- cold shower
- vitamins and/or meds
- sunbathing

- sauna
- send a "good morning" text
- learning something new
- declutter
- dance or sing to music
- meal planning
- listening to a podcast

add your own:

- ....
- ....
- ....
- ....
- ....
- ....
- ....
- ....
- ....

25 Evening Happiness Habits

An evening ritual is helpful to allow your body to relax and unwind and your mind to feel happy, at peace, and fulfilled. Ending your day intentionally is so powerful and can set you up for a great night's sleep and a successful next day. Here are some evening happiness habits I recommend to end the day right!

- prayer
- gratitude
- homemade dinner
- journaling
- 30 minutes of no tech
- mindful herbal tea
- dimming the lights
- listening to music
- reading
- going for a walk
- drinking water
- writing
- deep breathing
- vitamins and/or meds
- tidying up
- epsom salt bath
- sauna

- skin care routine
- calling a loved one
- quiet time
- exercise to destress
- intentional shower
- watching the sunset
- prepare for the next day
- pj's & downtime

add your own:

- ....
- ....
- ....
- ....
- ....
- ....
- ....

How to Use This Journal

When you meet someone who glistens with optimism, this is no accident. Habits that they commit to daily have helped them choose to feel good repeatedly until happiness is their natural disposition. And it's not just life circumstances that create happy people. Some of the happiest people I have met were not given an easier life. They learned to create strength and happiness from dark places. You can, too, starting right here!

WHAT TO EXPECT AS YOU BEGIN

This journal is a culmination of everything that helped me pull myself out of rock bottom and cultivate a positive mindset. Both the morning and evening entries will take only a few minutes to do, but as you stay consistent with them, they will have a cumulative effect on your life. You'll start seeing noticeable shifts in your thoughts, mindset, beliefs, and energy. You'll start to feel more optimistic, and you'll start attracting more positive experiences and people into your life.

While saturating your mind with positive affirmations and quotes can be a wonderful exercise in fostering happiness, reading positive messages daily is not often enough in creating real, lasting change within yourself. This is why participating fully in this journal and creating a routine filled with the happiness habits is so important.

To fully reap all the benefits of this book, I want you to make a commitment with me to show up every day. Make these entries a part of your self-care routine. Promise yourself that you'll do them every day, and then decide on the time and place in the morning and in the evening when you'll be completing the entries.

You might, for example, put this journal on your bedside table, and let it be the first thing you reach for in the morning and the last thing you do in the evening. You might place it on your kitchen table or desk, and do the morning entry as you have your morning coffee or before you start your work day. Whatever you decide, make it a priority to participate fully with the daily prompts and journal entries. If you do this, I promise to you that you will see positive shifts happening in your life within days.

Remember that nothing changes *if* nothing changes. If you truly want a happier life, this journal will help you take daily action toward this goal, so you can build new habits and new neural pathways that cultivate a happier, more fulfilling life.

HOW TO GET THE MOST OUT OF EACH ENTRY

Happy people have trained their minds to be happy and are consistent with their happiness habits. Each entry is full of inspiration and actionable steps that will instantly allow you to find happiness consistently. These are the same happiness habits that took me over a decade to learn and it's right here, done for you. All you need to do is show up. Don't wait for the motivation to be happy—create your own happiness!

MORNING INTENTIONS

Your morning routine is everything! It sets the tone for your day. It gives you the opportunity to start fresh. Research[3] also reveals that in the morning your brain waves are in a beta or gamma state, which is optimal for engaging and learning. What a great time to create new habits and thought patterns. Please complete each area with mindfulness and intention.

INSPIRATIONAL QUOTE: You will find a quote at the top of the page every morning to inspire and reinforce a forward-thinking mindset.

MENTAL HEALTH CHECK: This is your mood check-in to see how you feel at the start of your entry. Take a few moments to be in your body and document how you are feeling. Circle the emoji that matches your mood right now. Then, in the space next to it, complete the sentence "I want to feel _____." Developing this kind of emotional intelligence is a great indicator for success and happiness. Learning to recognize and accept how you feel is the key to letting go and moving toward better feelings.

GRATITUDE CHECK: Feeling thankful in the present moment is the key to happiness. Sure, everything may not be perfect, but there is still good in this moment. As deceptively simple as this exercise is, it may be the most powerful section of this journal and may have the biggest impact on your happiness.

DAILY AFFIRMATIONS: The words we use shape our reality. The more frequently we affirm something, the more ingrained it becomes in our subconscious mind, and the more we search for evidence of it in our life. In this section, I want you to create three affirmations for yourself that express something you want to accomplish. Be sure it's written as something you want, not what you don't want. For example, "I am financially abundant with multiple streams of income," rather than "I don't want debt." Also be sure your affirmations are in the present tense as though what you're stating is already true for you. And, lastly, create affirmations that make you feel excited and encouraged, not doubtful. They are *your* affirmations—make sure you believe in their possibility. Sometimes you need to build bridges for the things you don't yet believe can be possible by using phrases like, "I'm in the process of . . ." or "I'm learning to . . ." You will write one affirmation daily until you have fully embodied it, then you will create a new one in its place. Continue this cycle and enjoy the process! Affirmations help us enter a state of flow and align with our goals with less effort and more ease. *BONUS:* For faster results, practice reciting your affirmations in the mirror looking into your own eyes. Studies[4] find it's an effective way to boost self-acceptance—especially if your words and tone are compassionate and positive.

GOAL SETTING: Ask yourself, "What are three things I absolutely need to get done today?" Or, "What are three things I can do today that will move me closer to my goals?" Think of bite-size and easy-to-accomplish goals and then write them in the space provided. Research[5] shows that people who write down their goals are 42 percent more likely to achieve them than people who don't. That's why I've included a morning goal-setting routine after your affirmations.

SELF-CARE CHECK: As part of your self-care routine, I've included eight areas in which you can provide care and support for yourself. I'm not suggesting that you prioritize all of them in one day. These are listed in the morning so that you can check the ones you would like to prioritize that day. When you check the box, it does not have to mean that you have completed that item. It could also mean that you intend to prioritize it during the day, which allows you to reflect back on what you did during your evening entry for accountability. Do what you can. Don't feel the need to overdo it—this is self-care, after all!

THOUGHTS & NOTES: Please use this section to write out any additional ideas that come up during your entry. Some days you may find this area useful, other days you may not write anything at all, and other days you may write so much that you need to continue your thoughts in the blank pages in the back of this journal. Lean into what resonates each day and honor what wants to come out.

EVENING REFLECTIONS

Your evening routine is just as important as your morning one! As your day draws to a close, science says that your brain waves naturally start to slow down and you go from beta and alpha waves to theta[6]—which is optimal for dreaming and also learning. You can drastically change your life simply by taking charge of your evening routine. Let's engage your brain in a positive way and elevate your emotions right before bed! Please complete each area with mindfulness and intention.

INSPIRATIONAL QUOTE: Like the mornings, every evening also begins with inspiration or wisdom to reinforce positive beliefs. My goal here is to pick you up from wherever you might be at the end of your day. If some days you need more encouragement, don't forget the hundreds of thousands of free quote posters we have on our Power of Positivity social media channels and website.

GRATITUDE CHECK: This is your time to end the day with an attitude of gratitude. Every day may not be good, but there is something good in every day. Write it here.

WELLNESS CHECK: This is a place where I want you to celebrate. That's right, pat yourself on the back for all of the healthy choices you made. I know some days will be better than others, so don't get hung up on checking all the boxes; just pat yourself on the back for the ones you do. Remember: What you track expands!

MENTAL HEALTH CHECK: Most people are not in the habit of pausing, grounding in their body, and acknowledging how they truly feel. Take this opportunity to check in with yourself. Check several boxes if you need to. There are no right or wrong answers. If an emotion is interfering with your ability to relax for the evening, try one or a few of my evening happiness habits to help move through the emotion to provide relief. That's what I do!

HAPPINESS PROMPT: Happiness is a habit. It's a learned and practiced skill through the culmination of the right habits and mindset strategies. There are many things we can do to boost our mood and writing is a highly effective one. That's why I love journaling so much. Each happiness prompt—such as "The best advice you ever received is . . ."—changes daily and evokes an answer that has the ability to leave you a happier person.

WINS FOR THE DAY: Most dinner conversations are filled with what went wrong that day, mistakes that happened, or dramas that unfolded. I challenge you to instead focus on your wins. Ask yourself, "What went right?" Journal about it in the space provided. Then, share your wins at the dinner table. Encourage your family members to share theirs. Let's create a ripple of happiness within ourselves and to those we love by sharing what went right—no matter how small. A win is a win! When you focus on your wins, you give yourself permission to win more often.

THOUGHTS & NOTES: Please use this section to write about how your day went or anything else that might feel important in the moment. Some days, you may find this area useful, other days you may not write anything at all, and other days you may write so much that you need to continue your thoughts in the blank pages in the back of this journal. Lean into what resonates each day and honor what wants to come out. Don't forget what I always say: You can work through it if you *write* through it!

Wake up in the morning with purpose and passion and happiness will always follow.

I FEEL . . .    I WANT TO FEEL *energized*

💚 GRATITUDE CHECK

TODAY I AM GRATEFUL FOR . . .

1. *nature.*
2. *waking up healthy.*
3. *family and friends.*

TELL YOURSELF THIS TODAY: THE BETTER I FEEL ABOUT MY EXPERIENCES, THE BETTER MY EXPERIENCES BECOME!

💡 DAILY AFFIRMATIONS

1. *I am worthy of love and happiness.*
2. *I am financially secure.*
3. *I am full of joy, peace and love.*

BONUS: *Read each affirmation 10x in the mirror & throughout the day for faster results.*

☀ 3 PRIORITY GOALS

1. *important e-mails*
2. *monthly budget*
3. *calling loved ones*

Self-Care Check

- ✗ **PHYSICAL** Move or rest.
- ✗ **SOCIAL** Quality conversation.
- ✗ **SPIRITUAL** Good for the soul.
- ○ **HOUSEHOLD** Cleaning or organizing.
- ○ **PAMPERING** Treat yourself.
- ○ **PERSONAL** Time on a hobby.
- ✗ **EMOTIONAL** Honor feelings.
- ✗ **MENTAL** Read or learn.

💭 MY THOUGHTS & NOTES

I was feeling anxious, but gratitude, a nature walk and deep breaths alleviated it. Wow! Then a cup of tea and more deep breathing helped clear my mind. I am grateful.

When you find joy in the ordinary you are gifted more of the extraordinary.

💗 GRATITUDE CHECK

TONIGHT I AM GRATEFUL FOR . . .

1. a safe home.
2. loving people.
3. answered prayers.

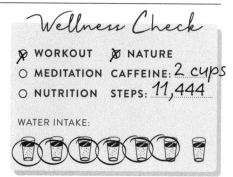

Wellness Check

☒ WORKOUT ☒ NATURE
○ MEDITATION CAFFEINE: 2 cups
○ NUTRITION STEPS: 11,444

WATER INTAKE:

🧠 MENTAL HEALTH CHECK

RIGHT NOW I FEEL . . . (YOU MAY CHOOSE MORE THAN ONE)

☒ HAPPY	○ PEACEFUL	○ PROUD
☒ LOVING	○ CREATIVE	○ SAD
☒ HOPEFUL	○ STRESSED	☒ TIRED
☒ CALM	○ ANNOYED	○ SCARED
○ ANGRY	○ POSITIVE	○ JOYFUL
○ OVERWHELMED	○ ANXIOUS	☒ grateful

THE BEST ADVICE YOU EVER RECEIVED IS . . .

Don't worry, trust that everything will work out.

🏆 WINS FOR THE DAY

TODAY I ACCOMPLISHED . . .

a nature hike/workout
eating well
a new revenue stream
memories w/a friend

☁ MY THOUGHTS & NOTES

I am so proud of myself for staying committed to my goals today. It feels good to honor myself. Self-care helps my self-image and mental health.

Wake up in the morning with purpose and passion and happiness will always follow.

I FEEL . . . 😃 😍 😴 🙁 😣 😖   I WANT TO FEEL ....

❤️ GRATITUDE CHECK

TODAY I AM GRATEFUL FOR . . .

1. ....

2. ....

3. ....

**TELL YOURSELF
THIS TODAY: THE
BETTER I FEEL ABOUT MY
EXPERIENCES, THE BETTER
MY EXPERIENCES BECOME!**

🔆 DAILY AFFIRMATIONS

1. ....

2. ....

3. ....

BONUS: *Read each affirmation 10x in the mirror & throughout the day for faster results.*

☀️ 3 PRIORITY GOALS

1. ....

2. ....

3. ....

Self-Care Check

○ **PHYSICAL**
Move or rest.

○ **SOCIAL**
Quality conversation.

○ **SPIRITUAL**
Good for the soul.

○ **HOUSEHOLD**
Cleaning or organizing.

○ **PAMPERING**
Treat yourself.

○ **PERSONAL**
Time on a hobby.

○ **EMOTIONAL**
Honor feelings.

○ **MENTAL**
Read or learn.

☁️ MY THOUGHTS & NOTES

....

....

....

....

....

EVENING REFLECTIONS

When you find joy in the ordinary you are gifted more of the extraordinary.

❤ GRATITUDE CHECK

TONIGHT I AM GRATEFUL FOR . . .

1. ....
2. ....
3. ....

🧠 MENTAL HEALTH CHECK

RIGHT NOW I FEEL . . . (YOU MAY CHOOSE MORE THAN ONE)

○ HAPPY	○ PEACEFUL	○ PROUD
○ LOVING	○ CREATIVE	○ SAD
○ HOPEFUL	○ STRESSED	○ TIRED
○ CALM	○ ANNOYED	○ SCARED
○ ANGRY	○ POSITIVE	○ JOYFUL
○ OVERWHELMED	○ ANXIOUS	○ ....

Wellness Check

○ WORKOUT   ○ NATURE
○ MEDITATION   CAFFEINE: ....
○ NUTRITION   STEPS: ....

WATER INTAKE:

THE BEST ADVICE YOU EVER
RECEIVED IS . . .

....
....
....
....

🏆 WINS FOR THE DAY

TODAY I ACCOMPLISHED . . .

....
....
....
....

💭 MY THOUGHTS & NOTES

....
....
....
....
....

Current Vibe: Saying YES to things that make me feel genuinely HAPPY!

I FEEL . . . 😄 😎 😐 😴 🙁 ☹️ 😣

I WANT TO FEEL ....

♡ GRATITUDE CHECK

TODAY I AM GRATEFUL FOR . . .

1. ....

2. ....

3. ....

WHAT ARE YOU PUTTING OFF UNTIL EVERYTHING IS JUST RIGHT? START PART OF IT TODAY! SMALL STEPS.

☀ DAILY AFFIRMATIONS

1. ....

2. ....

3. ....

BONUS: *Read each affirmation 10x in the mirror & throughout the day for faster results.*

☆ 3 PRIORITY GOALS

1. ....

2. ....

3. ....

Self-Care Check

○ **PHYSICAL**
Move or rest.

○ **SOCIAL**
Quality conversation.

○ **SPIRITUAL**
Good for the soul.

○ **HOUSEHOLD**
Cleaning or organizing.

○ **PAMPERING**
Treat yourself.

○ **PERSONAL**
Time on a hobby.

○ **EMOTIONAL**
Honor feelings.

○ **MENTAL**
Read or learn.

☁ MY THOUGHTS & NOTES

....

....

....

....

....

All you have is right now. Take a deep breath, silence your thoughts, and surrender to the moment.

🫶 GRATITUDE CHECK

TONIGHT I AM GRATEFUL FOR . . .

1. ....

2. ....

3. ....

Wellness Check

○ WORKOUT   ○ NATURE

○ MEDITATION   CAFFEINE: ....

○ NUTRITION   STEPS: ....

WATER INTAKE:

🧠 MENTAL HEALTH CHECK

RIGHT NOW I FEEL . . . (YOU MAY CHOOSE MORE THAN ONE)

○ HAPPY	○ PEACEFUL	○ PROUD
○ LOVING	○ CREATIVE	○ SAD
○ HOPEFUL	○ STRESSED	○ TIRED
○ CALM	○ ANNOYED	○ SCARED
○ ANGRY	○ POSITIVE	○ JOYFUL
○ OVERWHELMED	○ ANXIOUS	○ ....

WHAT BRAVE THING DID YOU DO TODAY?

....

....

....

....

🏆 WINS FOR THE DAY

TODAY I ACCOMPLISHED . . .

....

....

....

....

💭 MY THOUGHTS & NOTES

....

....

....

....

....

....

Happiness is a ripple effect. To be happy in the future, you have to decide to be happy right now.

I FEEL . . . 😄 😍 😐 😦 😩 😣   I WANT TO FEEL ....

♡ GRATITUDE CHECK

TODAY I AM GRATEFUL FOR . . .

1. ....
2. ....
3. ....

WHEN YOU ARE HAPPY, YOUR DOPAMINE LEVELS INCREASE NATURALLY. WHAT CAN YOU DO TODAY TO INFUSE YOURSELF WITH HAPPINESS?

💡 DAILY AFFIRMATIONS

1. ....
2. ....
3. ....

BONUS: *Read each affirmation 10x in the mirror & throughout the day for faster results.*

☀ 3 PRIORITY GOALS

1. ....
2. ....
3. ....

Self-Care Check

- ○ **PHYSICAL**
  Move or rest.
- ○ **SOCIAL**
  Quality conversation.
- ○ **SPIRITUAL**
  Good for the soul.
- ○ **HOUSEHOLD**
  Cleaning or organizing.
- ○ **PAMPERING**
  Treat yourself.
- ○ **PERSONAL**
  Time on a hobby.
- ○ **EMOTIONAL**
  Honor feelings.
- ○ **MENTAL**
  Read or learn.

💭 MY THOUGHTS & NOTES

....
....
....
....
....

EVENING REFLECTIONS

Never believe that a few caring people can't change the world.
—Margaret Mead

♡ GRATITUDE CHECK

TONIGHT I AM GRATEFUL FOR . . .

1. ....
2. ....
3. ....

🧠 MENTAL HEALTH CHECK

RIGHT NOW I FEEL . . . (YOU MAY CHOOSE MORE THAN ONE)

○ HAPPY	○ PEACEFUL	○ PROUD
○ LOVING	○ CREATIVE	○ SAD
○ HOPEFUL	○ STRESSED	○ TIRED
○ CALM	○ ANNOYED	○ SCARED
○ ANGRY	○ POSITIVE	○ JOYFUL
○ OVERWHELMED	○ ANXIOUS	○ ....

Wellness Check

○ WORKOUT   ○ NATURE
○ MEDITATION   CAFFEINE: ....
○ NUTRITION   STEPS: ....

WATER INTAKE:

🥛 🥛 🥛 🥛 🥛 🥛 🥛

WHAT'S YOUR FAVORITE THING ABOUT YOURSELF?

....
....
....

🏆 WINS FOR THE DAY

TODAY I ACCOMPLISHED . . .

....
....
....
....

💭 MY THOUGHTS & NOTES

....
....
....
....
....

Find meaning in everything and you will always find happiness.

___

I FEEL . . . 😄 😍 😐💤 🙁 😟 😣   I WANT TO FEEL ....

💟 GRATITUDE CHECK

TODAY I AM GRATEFUL FOR . . .

1. ....

2. ....

3. ....

**MAKE PLANS TODAY TO
SPEND TIME WITH PEOPLE
WHO ARE HEALTHY FOR
YOUR NERVOUS SYSTEM.**

🔆 DAILY AFFIRMATIONS

1. ....

2. ....

3. ....

BONUS: *Read each affirmation 10x in the mirror & throughout the day for faster results.*

☀ 3 PRIORITY GOALS

1. ....

2. ....

3. ....

Self-Care Check

○ **PHYSICAL**
Move or rest.

○ **SOCIAL**
Quality conversation.

○ **SPIRITUAL**
Good for the soul.

○ **HOUSEHOLD**
Cleaning or organizing.

○ **PAMPERING**
Treat yourself.

○ **PERSONAL**
Time on a hobby.

○ **EMOTIONAL**
Honor feelings.

○ **MENTAL**
Read or learn.

💭 MY THOUGHTS & NOTES

....

....

....

....

....

Your attitude and outlook on life determines your happiness,
not your circumstances.

♡ GRATITUDE CHECK

TONIGHT I AM GRATEFUL FOR . . .

1. ....

2. ....

3. ....

🧠 MENTAL HEALTH CHECK

RIGHT NOW I FEEL . . . (YOU MAY CHOOSE MORE THAN ONE)

○ HAPPY   ○ PEACEFUL   ○ PROUD
○ LOVING   ○ CREATIVE   ○ SAD
○ HOPEFUL   ○ STRESSED   ○ TIRED
○ CALM   ○ ANNOYED   ○ SCARED
○ ANGRY   ○ POSITIVE   ○ JOYFUL
○ OVERWHELMED   ○ ANXIOUS   ○ ....

Wellness Check

○ WORKOUT   ○ NATURE
○ MEDITATION CAFFEINE: ....
○ NUTRITION   STEPS: ....

WATER INTAKE:

□ □ □ □ □ □ □

IF YOU COULD GIVE SOMEONE A
PIECE OF ADVICE, WHAT WOULD
IT BE?

....
....
....

🏆 WINS FOR THE DAY

TODAY I ACCOMPLISHED . . .

....
....
....
....

☁ MY THOUGHTS & NOTES

....
....
....
....
....

Think positive as often as you can and you will be filled with moments worth celebrating.

I FEEL . . . 😃 😍 😴 ☹️ 😢 😠   I WANT TO FEEL ....

❤️ GRATITUDE CHECK

TODAY I AM GRATEFUL FOR . . .

1. ....

2. ....

3. ....

**THINK OF 3 THINGS YOU
CAN DO TO BRING JOY
INTO YOUR DAY
. . . GO!**

💡 DAILY AFFIRMATIONS

1. ....

2. ....

3. ....

BONUS: *Read each affirmation 10x in the mirror & throughout the day for faster results.*

☆ 3 PRIORITY GOALS

1. ....

2. ....

3. ....

💭 MY THOUGHTS & NOTES

Self-Care Check

○ **PHYSICAL**
Move or rest.

○ **SOCIAL**
Quality conversation.

○ **SPIRITUAL**
Good for the soul.

○ **HOUSEHOLD**
Cleaning or organizing.

○ **PAMPERING**
Treat yourself.

○ **PERSONAL**
Time on a hobby.

○ **EMOTIONAL**
Honor feelings.

○ **MENTAL**
Read or learn.

....

....

....

....

....

EVENING REFLECTIONS

I just think happiness is what makes you pretty. Period.
Happy people are beautiful. —Drew Barrymore

GRATITUDE CHECK

TONIGHT I AM GRATEFUL FOR . . .

1. ....

2. ....

3. ....

MENTAL HEALTH CHECK

RIGHT NOW I FEEL . . . (YOU MAY CHOOSE MORE THAN ONE)

○ HAPPY	○ PEACEFUL	○ PROUD
○ LOVING	○ CREATIVE	○ SAD
○ HOPEFUL	○ STRESSED	○ TIRED
○ CALM	○ ANNOYED	○ SCARED
○ ANGRY	○ POSITIVE	○ JOYFUL
○ OVERWHELMED	○ ANXIOUS	○ ....

Wellness Check

○ WORKOUT   ○ NATURE
○ MEDITATION   CAFFEINE: ....
○ NUTRITION   STEPS: ....

WATER INTAKE:

WHAT IMPROVED YOUR QUALITY
OF LIFE SO MUCH THAT YOU
WISH YOU DID IT SOONER?

....

....

....

WINS FOR THE DAY

TODAY I ACCOMPLISHED . . .

....

....

....

....

MY THOUGHTS & NOTES

....

....

....

....

....

When we focus on our wins, we give ourselves permission to win more often.

I FEEL . . . 😀 😍 😴 🙁 😟 😣   I WANT TO FEEL ....

❤️ GRATITUDE CHECK

TODAY I AM GRATEFUL FOR . . .

1. ....

2. ....

3. ....

**TODAY, MAKE CHOICES
FROM A PLACE OF PEACE
AND JOY, NOT FEAR.**

💡 DAILY AFFIRMATIONS

1. ....

2. ....

3. ....

BONUS: *Read each affirmation 10x in the mirror & throughout the day for faster results.*

☀️ 3 PRIORITY GOALS

1. ....

2. ....

3. ....

💭 MY THOUGHTS & NOTES

Self-Care Check

○ **PHYSICAL**
Move or rest.

○ **SOCIAL**
Quality conversation.

○ **SPIRITUAL**
Good for the soul.

○ **HOUSEHOLD**
Cleaning or organizing.

○ **PAMPERING**
Treat yourself.

○ **PERSONAL**
Time on a hobby.

○ **EMOTIONAL**
Honor feelings.

○ **MENTAL**
Read or learn.

....
....
....
....
....

Note to self: My feelings are valid. It's okay to allow myself to heal and be happy again.

🌿 GRATITUDE CHECK

TONIGHT I AM GRATEFUL FOR ...

1. ....
2. ....
3. ....

Wellness Check

- ○ WORKOUT   ○ NATURE
- ○ MEDITATION CAFFEINE: ....
- ○ NUTRITION   STEPS: ....

WATER INTAKE:

🧠 MENTAL HEALTH CHECK

RIGHT NOW I FEEL ... (YOU MAY CHOOSE MORE THAN ONE)

○ HAPPY	○ PEACEFUL	○ PROUD
○ LOVING	○ CREATIVE	○ SAD
○ HOPEFUL	○ STRESSED	○ TIRED
○ CALM	○ ANNOYED	○ SCARED
○ ANGRY	○ POSITIVE	○ JOYFUL
○ OVERWHELMED	○ ANXIOUS	○ ....

DO YOU LIVE BY ANY PIECE OF ADVICE OR MOTTO?

....
....
....

🏆 WINS FOR THE DAY

TODAY I ACCOMPLISHED ...

....
....
....

💭 MY THOUGHTS & NOTES

....
....
....
....
....

Don't judge each day by the harvest you reap but by the seeds that you plant. —Robert Louis Stevenson

I FEEL . . . 😄 😍 😴 🙁 😟 😖   I WANT TO FEEL ....

💗 GRATITUDE CHECK

TODAY I AM GRATEFUL FOR . . .

1. ....

2. ....

3. ....

IS THERE SOMETHING THAT YOU COULD DO FOR SOMEONE TODAY THAT WOULD MAKE THEM FEEL LIKE IT'S THEIR LUCKY DAY? DO IT!

💡 DAILY AFFIRMATIONS

1. ....

2. ....

3. ....

BONUS: *Read each affirmation 10x in the mirror & throughout the day for faster results.*

☆ 3 PRIORITY GOALS

1. ....

2. ....

3. ....

Self-Care Check

○ **PHYSICAL**
Move or rest.

○ **SOCIAL**
Quality conversation.

○ **SPIRITUAL**
Good for the soul.

○ **HOUSEHOLD**
Cleaning or organizing.

○ **PAMPERING**
Treat yourself.

○ **PERSONAL**
Time on a hobby.

○ **EMOTIONAL**
Honor feelings.

○ **MENTAL**
Read or learn.

💭 MY THOUGHTS & NOTES

....

....

....

....

....

....

If you're dealing with something heavy, remember this:
Change is necessary to release negativity for good.

♡ GRATITUDE CHECK

TONIGHT I AM GRATEFUL FOR . . .

1. ....

2. ....

3. ....

🧠 MENTAL HEALTH CHECK

RIGHT NOW I FEEL . . . (YOU MAY CHOOSE MORE THAN ONE)

○ HAPPY	○ PEACEFUL	○ PROUD
○ LOVING	○ CREATIVE	○ SAD
○ HOPEFUL	○ STRESSED	○ TIRED
○ CALM	○ ANNOYED	○ SCARED
○ ANGRY	○ POSITIVE	○ JOYFUL
○ OVERWHELMED	○ ANXIOUS	○ ....

Wellness Check

○ WORKOUT   ○ NATURE

○ MEDITATION   CAFFEINE: ....

○ NUTRITION   STEPS: ....

WATER INTAKE:

WHAT'S SOMETHING YOU
LOOK FORWARD TO EVERY
SINGLE DAY?

....

....

....

🏆 WINS FOR THE DAY

TODAY I ACCOMPLISHED . . .

....

....

....

....

☁ MY THOUGHTS & NOTES

....

....

....

....

....

There is nothing you have to do, get, or be in order to be happy.
—Srikumar Rao

I FEEL . . . 😃 😍 😑 😦 😣 😖   I WANT TO FEEL ....

♡ GRATITUDE CHECK

TODAY I AM GRATEFUL FOR . . .

1. ....
2. ....
3. ....

**BE MINDFUL AND PAY
ATTENTION TO HOW
HAPPINESS FEELS INSIDE
YOUR BODY.**

☼ DAILY AFFIRMATIONS

1. ....
2. ....
3. ....

BONUS: *Read each affirmation 10x in the mirror & throughout the day for faster results.*

☼ 3 PRIORITY GOALS

1. ....
2. ....
3. ....

Self-Care Check

- ○ **PHYSICAL**
  Move or rest.
- ○ **SOCIAL**
  Quality conversation.
- ○ **SPIRITUAL**
  Good for the soul.
- ○ **HOUSEHOLD**
  Cleaning or organizing.
- ○ **PAMPERING**
  Treat yourself.
- ○ **PERSONAL**
  Time on a hobby.
- ○ **EMOTIONAL**
  Honor feelings.
- ○ **MENTAL**
  Read or learn.

☁ MY THOUGHTS & NOTES

....
....
....
....
....

You have the power to live the life of your dreams, but you are the only driver with the exact coordinates.

🫀 GRATITUDE CHECK

TONIGHT I AM GRATEFUL FOR . . .

1. ....

2. ....

3. ....

Wellness Check

- ○ WORKOUT   ○ NATURE
- ○ MEDITATION   CAFFEINE: ....
- ○ NUTRITION   STEPS: ....

WATER INTAKE:

🧠 MENTAL HEALTH CHECK

RIGHT NOW I FEEL . . . (YOU MAY CHOOSE MORE THAN ONE)

○ HAPPY	○ PEACEFUL	○ PROUD
○ LOVING	○ CREATIVE	○ SAD
○ HOPEFUL	○ STRESSED	○ TIRED
○ CALM	○ ANNOYED	○ SCARED
○ ANGRY	○ POSITIVE	○ JOYFUL
○ OVERWHELMED	○ ANXIOUS	○ ....

WHAT'S A SIMPLE HABIT YOU PRACTICE DAILY THAT HELPS YOU STAY PEACEFUL?

....

....

....

🏆 WINS FOR THE DAY

TODAY I ACCOMPLISHED . . .

....

....

....

....

💭 MY THOUGHTS & NOTES

....

....

....

....

....

When you help others, you help yourself. Kindness is at the heart of happiness.

I FEEL . . . 😃 😍 😴 ☹️ 😣 😠   I WANT TO FEEL ....

🫶 GRATITUDE CHECK

TODAY I AM GRATEFUL FOR . . .

1. ....
2. ....
3. ....

IF YOU ONLY HAD 24 HOURS LEFT ON THIS EARTH, WHO WOULD YOU CONNECT WITH? IF YOU CAN, CHECK IN AND PRIORITIZE TIME WITH THEM TODAY!

💡 DAILY AFFIRMATIONS

1. ....
2. ....
3. ....

BONUS: *Read each affirmation 10x in the mirror & throughout the day for faster results.*

☀️ 3 PRIORITY GOALS

1. ....
2. ....
3. ....

💭 MY THOUGHTS & NOTES

Self-Care Check

○ **PHYSICAL**
Move or rest.

○ **SOCIAL**
Quality conversation.

○ **SPIRITUAL**
Good for the soul.

○ **HOUSEHOLD**
Cleaning or organizing.

○ **PAMPERING**
Treat yourself.

○ **PERSONAL**
Time on a hobby.

○ **EMOTIONAL**
Honor feelings.

○ **MENTAL**
Read or learn.

....
....
....
....

EVENING REFLECTIONS

Tough times never last, but tough people do. —Robert H. Schuller

GRATITUDE CHECK

TONIGHT I AM GRATEFUL FOR . . .

1. ....
2. ....
3. ....

Wellness Check

- ○ WORKOUT ○ NATURE
- ○ MEDITATION CAFFEINE: ....
- ○ NUTRITION STEPS: ....

WATER INTAKE:

MENTAL HEALTH CHECK

RIGHT NOW I FEEL . . . (YOU MAY CHOOSE MORE THAN ONE)

○ HAPPY	○ PEACEFUL	○ PROUD
○ LOVING	○ CREATIVE	○ SAD
○ HOPEFUL	○ STRESSED	○ TIRED
○ CALM	○ ANNOYED	○ SCARED
○ ANGRY	○ POSITIVE	○ JOYFUL
○ OVERWHELMED	○ ANXIOUS	○ ....

DESCRIBE YOUR IDEA OF A
GREAT DAY . . .

WINS FOR THE DAY

TODAY I ACCOMPLISHED . . .

MY THOUGHTS & NOTES

By recording your dreams and goals on paper, you set in motion the process of becoming the person you most want to be. —Mark Victor Hansen

I FEEL . . . 😄 😍 😴 ☹️ 😢 😖   I WANT TO FEEL ....

💗 GRATITUDE CHECK

TODAY I AM GRATEFUL FOR . . .

1. ....
2. ....
3. ....

TAKE A DEEP BREATH AND THINK ABOUT WHAT HAPPINESS FEELS LIKE TO YOU. WHAT ARE YOU DOING? WHO IS THERE? HONOR THAT FEELING TODAY!

💡 DAILY AFFIRMATIONS

1. ....
2. ....
3. ....

BONUS: *Read each affirmation 10x in the mirror & throughout the day for faster results.*

☀️ 3 PRIORITY GOALS

1. ....
2. ....
3. ....

💭 MY THOUGHTS & NOTES

Self-Care Check

○ **PHYSICAL**
Move or rest.

○ **SOCIAL**
Quality conversation.

○ **SPIRITUAL**
Good for the soul.

○ **HOUSEHOLD**
Cleaning or organizing.

○ **PAMPERING**
Treat yourself.

○ **PERSONAL**
Time on a hobby.

○ **EMOTIONAL**
Honor feelings.

○ **MENTAL**
Read or learn.

....
....
....
....
....

You can train yourself to focus on the positive aspects of anything. That's where your power lies.

♡ GRATITUDE CHECK

TONIGHT I AM GRATEFUL FOR . . .

1. ....

2. ....

3. ....

Wellness Check

- ○ WORKOUT   ○ NATURE
- ○ MEDITATION   CAFFEINE: ....
- ○ NUTRITION   STEPS: ....

WATER INTAKE:

🥛 🥛 🥛 🥛 🥛 🥛 🥛

🧠 MENTAL HEALTH CHECK

RIGHT NOW I FEEL . . . (YOU MAY CHOOSE MORE THAN ONE)

○ HAPPY	○ PEACEFUL	○ PROUD
○ LOVING	○ CREATIVE	○ SAD
○ HOPEFUL	○ STRESSED	○ TIRED
○ CALM	○ ANNOYED	○ SCARED
○ ANGRY	○ POSITIVE	○ JOYFUL
○ OVERWHELMED	○ ANXIOUS	○ ....

WHAT BRINGS YOU THE MOST JOY RIGHT NOW?

....

....

....

🏆 WINS FOR THE DAY

TODAY I ACCOMPLISHED . . .

....

....

....

....

💭 MY THOUGHTS & NOTES

....

....

....

....

....

Make your whole day a constant, silent prayer of thanks and watch your life change.

I FEEL . . . 😃 😍 😐 😦 😢 😣   I WANT TO FEEL ....

♡ GRATITUDE CHECK

TODAY I AM GRATEFUL FOR . . .

1. ....
2. ....
3. ....

WE LEARN BEST THROUGH PLAY. HOW CAN YOU MAKE YOUR WORK TODAY FUN?

☼ DAILY AFFIRMATIONS

1. ....
2. ....
3. ....

BONUS: *Read each affirmation 10x in the mirror & throughout the day for faster results.*

☼ 3 PRIORITY GOALS

1. ....
2. ....
3. ....

Self-Care Check

- ○ **PHYSICAL**
  Move or rest.
- ○ **SOCIAL**
  Quality conversation.
- ○ **SPIRITUAL**
  Good for the soul.
- ○ **HOUSEHOLD**
  Cleaning or organizing.
- ○ **PAMPERING**
  Treat yourself.
- ○ **PERSONAL**
  Time on a hobby.
- ○ **EMOTIONAL**
  Honor feelings.
- ○ **MENTAL**
  Read or learn.

☁ MY THOUGHTS & NOTES

....
....
....
....
....

Be a vessel of change with this affirmation: I only harbor loving thoughts about myself and others.

GRATITUDE CHECK

TONIGHT I AM GRATEFUL FOR . . .

1. ....

2. ....

3. ....

Wellness Check

- O WORKOUT   O NATURE
- O MEDITATION   CAFFEINE: ....
- O NUTRITION   STEPS: ....

WATER INTAKE:

MENTAL HEALTH CHECK

RIGHT NOW I FEEL . . . (YOU MAY CHOOSE MORE THAN ONE)

O HAPPY	O PEACEFUL	O PROUD
O LOVING	O CREATIVE	O SAD
O HOPEFUL	O STRESSED	O TIRED
O CALM	O ANNOYED	O SCARED
O ANGRY	O POSITIVE	O JOYFUL
O OVERWHELMED	O ANXIOUS	O ....

EVENING GRATITUDE CHECK!
LIST 3 THINGS YOU ARE
GRATEFUL FOR TODAY . . .

....

....

....

WINS FOR THE DAY

TODAY I ACCOMPLISHED . . .

....

....

....

....

MY THOUGHTS & NOTES

....

....

....

....

....

....

A joyful heart is good medicine, but a crushed spirit dries up the bones. —Proverbs 17:22

I FEEL ... 😄😍😴🙁😢😣   I WANT TO FEEL ....

🫶 GRATITUDE CHECK

TODAY I AM GRATEFUL FOR ...

1. ....

2. ....

3. ....

**WHAT IS SOMETHING THAT
YOU COULD DO TODAY
THAT WOULD UNLOCK
MORE HAPPINESS?**

🔅 DAILY AFFIRMATIONS

1. ....

2. ....

3. ....

BONUS: *Read each affirmation 10x in the mirror & throughout the day for faster results.*

🔅 3 PRIORITY GOALS

1. ....

2. ....

3. ....

Self-Care Check

○ **PHYSICAL**   ○ **SOCIAL**
Move or rest.   Quality conversation.

○ **SPIRITUAL**   ○ **HOUSEHOLD**
Good for the soul.   Cleaning or organizing.

○ **PAMPERING**   ○ **PERSONAL**
Treat yourself.   Time on a hobby.

○ **EMOTIONAL**   ○ **MENTAL**
Honor feelings.   Read or learn.

💭 MY THOUGHTS & NOTES

....

....

....

....

....

EVENING REFLECTIONS

Neurons that fire together, wire together. —Donald Hebb

❤️ GRATITUDE CHECK

TONIGHT I AM GRATEFUL FOR . . .

1. ....

2. ....

3. ....

Wellness Check

○ WORKOUT ○ NATURE

○ MEDITATION CAFFEINE: ....

○ NUTRITION STEPS: ....

WATER INTAKE:

🧠 MENTAL HEALTH CHECK

RIGHT NOW I FEEL . . . (YOU MAY CHOOSE MORE THAN ONE)

○ HAPPY	○ PEACEFUL	○ PROUD
○ LOVING	○ CREATIVE	○ SAD
○ HOPEFUL	○ STRESSED	○ TIRED
○ CALM	○ ANNOYED	○ SCARED
○ ANGRY	○ POSITIVE	○ JOYFUL
○ OVERWHELMED	○ ANXIOUS	○ ....

WHAT FAMILY TRADITIONS DID YOU HAVE AS A CHILD THAT YOU ARE STILL THANKFUL FOR?

....

....

....

🏆 WINS FOR THE DAY

TODAY I ACCOMPLISHED . . .

....

....

....

....

💭 MY THOUGHTS & NOTES

....

....

....

....

....

....

Don't let a little negativity keep you from seeing all the good that also can happen today!

I FEEL ... 😀 😍 😑 🙁 ☹️ 😣   I WANT TO FEEL ....

🌱 GRATITUDE CHECK

TODAY I AM GRATEFUL FOR . . .

1. ....

2. ....

3. ....

**THINK OF SOMEONE
YOU KNOW WHO HAS AN
AMAZING SKILL OR GIFT.
CALL OR TEXT THEM TODAY
AND SHARE WHY YOU
ADMIRE THEM.**

💡 DAILY AFFIRMATIONS

1. ....

2. ....

3. ....

BONUS: *Read each affirmation 10x in the mirror & throughout the day for faster results.*

☀️ 3 PRIORITY GOALS

1. ....

2. ....

3. ....

💭 MY THOUGHTS & NOTES

Self-Care Check

○ **PHYSICAL**
Move or rest.

○ **SOCIAL**
Quality conversation.

○ **SPIRITUAL**
Good for the soul.

○ **HOUSEHOLD**
Cleaning or organizing.

○ **PAMPERING**
Treat yourself.

○ **PERSONAL**
Time on a hobby.

○ **EMOTIONAL**
Honor feelings.

○ **MENTAL**
Read or learn.

....

....

....

....

....

Happiness is when you genuinely feel good about yourself, without the need to prove it to anyone.

GRATITUDE CHECK

TONIGHT I AM GRATEFUL FOR . . .

1. ....

2. ....

3. ....

Wellness Check

- ○ WORKOUT   ○ NATURE
- ○ MEDITATION   CAFFEINE: ....
- ○ NUTRITION   STEPS: ....

WATER INTAKE:

MENTAL HEALTH CHECK

RIGHT NOW I FEEL . . . (YOU MAY CHOOSE MORE THAN ONE)

○ HAPPY	○ PEACEFUL	○ PROUD
○ LOVING	○ CREATIVE	○ SAD
○ HOPEFUL	○ STRESSED	○ TIRED
○ CALM	○ ANNOYED	○ SCARED
○ ANGRY	○ POSITIVE	○ JOYFUL
○ OVERWHELMED	○ ANXIOUS	○ ....

IN TIMES OF STRESS, WHAT GETS YOU THROUGH?

....

....

....

WINS FOR THE DAY

TODAY I ACCOMPLISHED . . .

....

....

....

....

MY THOUGHTS & NOTES

....

....

....

....

....

MORNING INTENTIONS

DATE: .... / .... / ....

You are strong enough to face whatever comes your way today, even if it doesn't feel like it right now.

I FEEL . . . 😄 😍 😑💤 ☹️ 😣 😫   I WANT TO FEEL ....

🫶 GRATITUDE CHECK

TODAY I AM GRATEFUL FOR . . .

1. ....
2. ....
3. ....

**TODAY, BE AS
COMPASSIONATE TO
YOURSELF AS YOU WOULD
BE TO A GOOD FRIEND.**

💡 DAILY AFFIRMATIONS

1. ....
2. ....
3. ....

BONUS: *Read each affirmation 10x in the mirror & throughout the day for faster results.*

☆ 3 PRIORITY GOALS

1. ....
2. ....
3. ....

💭 MY THOUGHTS & NOTES

Self-Care Check

○ **PHYSICAL**
Move or rest.

○ **SOCIAL**
Quality conversation.

○ **SPIRITUAL**
Good for the soul.

○ **HOUSEHOLD**
Cleaning or organizing.

○ **PAMPERING**
Treat yourself.

○ **PERSONAL**
Time on a hobby.

○ **EMOTIONAL**
Honor feelings.

○ **MENTAL**
Read or learn.

....
....
....
....
....

Focus your energy on everything that feeds your purpose, deepens your peace, and fuels a positive mindset. —Lewis Howes

GRATITUDE CHECK

TONIGHT I AM GRATEFUL FOR . . .

1. ....
2. ....
3. ....

Wellness Check

○ WORKOUT   ○ NATURE
○ MEDITATION CAFFEINE: ....
○ NUTRITION   STEPS: ....

WATER INTAKE:

MENTAL HEALTH CHECK

RIGHT NOW I FEEL . . . (YOU MAY CHOOSE MORE THAN ONE)

○ HAPPY	○ PEACEFUL	○ PROUD
○ LOVING	○ CREATIVE	○ SAD
○ HOPEFUL	○ STRESSED	○ TIRED
○ CALM	○ ANNOYED	○ SCARED
○ ANGRY	○ POSITIVE	○ JOYFUL
○ OVERWHELMED	○ ANXIOUS	○ ....

WRITE DOWN 3 THINGS THAT MAKE YOU LAUGH . . . THEN TAKE TIME FOR ONE OF THEM!

....
....
....

WINS FOR THE DAY

TODAY I ACCOMPLISHED . . .

....
....
....
....

MY THOUGHTS & NOTES

....
....
....
....
....

Note to self: Having healthy boundaries is an important part of my happiness.

I FEEL . . . 😄 😍 😔 🙁 ☹️ 😣   I WANT TO FEEL ....

🫶 GRATITUDE CHECK

TODAY I AM GRATEFUL FOR . . .

1. ....

2. ....

3. ....

DON'T SETTLE OR GIVE IN JUST TO PLEASE SOMEONE WHEN IT DOESN'T FEEL RIGHT INSIDE. LISTEN TO YOUR INTUITION!

💡 DAILY AFFIRMATIONS

1. ....

2. ....

3. ....

BONUS: *Read each affirmation 10x in the mirror & throughout the day for faster results.*

☀️ 3 PRIORITY GOALS

1. ....

2. ....

3. ....

Self-Care Check

- ○ **PHYSICAL**
  Move or rest.
- ○ **SOCIAL**
  Quality conversation.
- ○ **SPIRITUAL**
  Good for the soul.
- ○ **HOUSEHOLD**
  Cleaning or organizing.
- ○ **PAMPERING**
  Treat yourself.
- ○ **PERSONAL**
  Time on a hobby.
- ○ **EMOTIONAL**
  Honor feelings.
- ○ **MENTAL**
  Read or learn.

💭 MY THOUGHTS & NOTES

....

....

....

....

....

EVENING REFLECTIONS

I believe that tomorrow is another day and I believe in miracles.
—Audrey Hepburn

❤ GRATITUDE CHECK

TONIGHT I AM GRATEFUL FOR . . .

1. ....

2. ....

3. ....

Wellness Check

○ WORKOUT   ○ NATURE

○ MEDITATION   CAFFEINE: ....

○ NUTRITION   STEPS: ....

WATER INTAKE:

🧠 MENTAL HEALTH CHECK

RIGHT NOW I FEEL . . . (YOU MAY CHOOSE MORE THAN ONE)

○ HAPPY	○ PEACEFUL	○ PROUD
○ LOVING	○ CREATIVE	○ SAD
○ HOPEFUL	○ STRESSED	○ TIRED
○ CALM	○ ANNOYED	○ SCARED
○ ANGRY	○ POSITIVE	○ JOYFUL
○ OVERWHELMED	○ ANXIOUS	○ ....

WHAT ADVICE WOULD YOU GIVE
TO YOUR YOUNGER SELF?

🏆 WINS FOR THE DAY

TODAY I ACCOMPLISHED . . .

☁ MY THOUGHTS & NOTES

Remember, as long as you are breathing it's never too late to start a new beginning.

I FEEL . . . 😊 😍 😴 🙁 ☹️ 😣   I WANT TO FEEL ....

💟 GRATITUDE CHECK

TODAY I AM GRATEFUL FOR . . .

1. ....

2. ....

3. ....

WHEN YOU LIVE FROM A GRATEFUL HEART, EVERYTHING YOU "HAVE TO" DO STARTS TO SHIFT INTO THINGS YOU "GET TO" DO.

💡 DAILY AFFIRMATIONS

1. ....

2. ....

3. ....

BONUS: *Read each affirmation 10x in the mirror & throughout the day for faster results.*

☀️ 3 PRIORITY GOALS

1. ....

2. ....

3. ....

💭 MY THOUGHTS & NOTES

Self-Care Check

○ **PHYSICAL**
Move or rest.

○ **SOCIAL**
Quality conversation.

○ **SPIRITUAL**
Good for the soul.

○ **HOUSEHOLD**
Cleaning or organizing.

○ **PAMPERING**
Treat yourself.

○ **PERSONAL**
Time on a hobby.

○ **EMOTIONAL**
Honor feelings.

○ **MENTAL**
Read or learn.

....

....

....

....

....

....

EVENING REFLECTIONS

Happiness is not about getting everything you want, it's about enjoying all that you have.

♡ GRATITUDE CHECK

TONIGHT I AM GRATEFUL FOR . . .

1. ....

2. ....

3. ....

🧠 MENTAL HEALTH CHECK

RIGHT NOW I FEEL . . . (YOU MAY CHOOSE MORE THAN ONE)

○ HAPPY	○ PEACEFUL	○ PROUD
○ LOVING	○ CREATIVE	○ SAD
○ HOPEFUL	○ STRESSED	○ TIRED
○ CALM	○ ANNOYED	○ SCARED
○ ANGRY	○ POSITIVE	○ JOYFUL
○ OVERWHELMED	○ ANXIOUS	○ ....

Wellness Check

○ WORKOUT   ○ NATURE

○ MEDITATION   CAFFEINE: ....

○ NUTRITION   STEPS: ....

WATER INTAKE:

🥛 🥛 🥛 🥛 🥛 🥛 🥛

WHAT DOES KINDNESS MEAN TO YOU?

....

....

....

🏆 WINS FOR THE DAY

TODAY I ACCOMPLISHED . . .

....

....

....

....

💭 MY THOUGHTS & NOTES

....

....

....

....

....

When you do things from your soul, you feel a river moving in you, a joy. —Rumi

I FEEL . . . 😄 😍 😑 ☹️ 😢 😣   I WANT TO FEEL ....

❤️ GRATITUDE CHECK

TODAY I AM GRATEFUL FOR . . .

1. ....

2. ....

3. ....

TODAY, KEEP YOUR FOCUS ON THE GOOD BY INTENTIONALLY THINKING, FEELING, AND SPEAKING POSITIVE THOUGHTS.

💡 DAILY AFFIRMATIONS

1. ....

2. ....

3. ....

BONUS: *Read each affirmation 10x in the mirror & throughout the day for faster results.*

☀️ 3 PRIORITY GOALS

1. ....

2. ....

3. ....

💭 MY THOUGHTS & NOTES

Self-Care Check

○ **PHYSICAL**
Move or rest.

○ **SOCIAL**
Quality conversation.

○ **SPIRITUAL**
Good for the soul.

○ **HOUSEHOLD**
Cleaning or organizing.

○ **PAMPERING**
Treat yourself.

○ **PERSONAL**
Time on a hobby.

○ **EMOTIONAL**
Honor feelings.

○ **MENTAL**
Read or learn.

....
....
....
....
....

The smile on my face does not mean my life is perfect. It means that despite my challenges, I choose to focus on my blessings.

♡ GRATITUDE CHECK

TONIGHT I AM GRATEFUL FOR . . .

1. ....
2. ....
3. ....

🧠 MENTAL HEALTH CHECK

RIGHT NOW I FEEL . . . (YOU MAY CHOOSE MORE THAN ONE)

○ HAPPY	○ PEACEFUL	○ PROUD
○ LOVING	○ CREATIVE	○ SAD
○ HOPEFUL	○ STRESSED	○ TIRED
○ CALM	○ ANNOYED	○ SCARED
○ ANGRY	○ POSITIVE	○ JOYFUL
○ OVERWHELMED	○ ANXIOUS	○ ....

Wellness Check

○ WORKOUT   ○ NATURE
○ MEDITATION   CAFFEINE: ....
○ NUTRITION   STEPS: ....

WATER INTAKE:

🥛 🥛 🥛 🥛 🥛 🥛 🥛

WHAT THING(S) DID YOUR MOTHER/FATHER ALWAYS SAY THAT HELPED YOU?

....
....
....

🏆 WINS FOR THE DAY

TODAY I ACCOMPLISHED . . .

....
....
....
....

💭 MY THOUGHTS & NOTES

....
....
....
....
....

Sometimes you have to stop thinking so much and go where your heart takes you.

I FEEL . . . 😄 😍 😑 😦 😣 😫   I WANT TO FEEL ....

🌹 GRATITUDE CHECK

TODAY I AM GRATEFUL FOR . . .

1. ....
2. ....
3. ....

IF YOU VEER OFF COURSE TODAY, BE GENTLE WITH YOURSELF AND REDIRECT. DURING CHALLENGING MOMENTS, USE GRATITUDE TO CHANGE THE MOMENTUM.

💡 DAILY AFFIRMATIONS

1. ....
2. ....
3. ....

BONUS: *Read each affirmation 10x in the mirror & throughout the day for faster results.*

☼ 3 PRIORITY GOALS

1. ....
2. ....
3. ....

Self-Care Check

○ **PHYSICAL**
Move or rest.

○ **SOCIAL**
Quality conversation.

○ **SPIRITUAL**
Good for the soul.

○ **HOUSEHOLD**
Cleaning or organizing.

○ **PAMPERING**
Treat yourself.

○ **PERSONAL**
Time on a hobby.

○ **EMOTIONAL**
Honor feelings.

○ **MENTAL**
Read or learn.

☁ MY THOUGHTS & NOTES

....
....
....
....
....

EVENING REFLECTIONS

Reminder: You are always responsible for how you act, no matter how you feel.

♡ GRATITUDE CHECK

TONIGHT I AM GRATEFUL FOR . . .

1. ....
2. ....
3. ....

Wellness Check

- ○ **WORKOUT**   ○ **NATURE**
- ○ **MEDITATION**   **CAFFEINE:** ....
- ○ **NUTRITION**   **STEPS:** ....

WATER INTAKE:

🧠 MENTAL HEALTH CHECK

RIGHT NOW I FEEL . . . (YOU MAY CHOOSE MORE THAN ONE)

○ HAPPY	○ PEACEFUL	○ PROUD
○ LOVING	○ CREATIVE	○ SAD
○ HOPEFUL	○ STRESSED	○ TIRED
○ CALM	○ ANNOYED	○ SCARED
○ ANGRY	○ POSITIVE	○ JOYFUL
○ OVERWHELMED	○ ANXIOUS	○ ....

WHAT MOVIE OR BOOK IMPACTED THE WAY YOU LIVE YOUR LIFE? WHY?

....
....
....

🏆 WINS FOR THE DAY

TODAY I ACCOMPLISHED . . .

....
....
....
....

💭 MY THOUGHTS & NOTES

....
....
....
....
....

MORNING INTENTIONS

One small positive thought can change the direction of the whole day.

I FEEL . . . 😃 😍 😴 🙁 😣 😖   I WANT TO FEEL ....

❤️ GRATITUDE CHECK

TODAY I AM GRATEFUL FOR . . .

1. ....

2. ....

3. ....

GRIEF CAN STEAL OUR HAPPINESS UNLESS WE FLIP THE SCRIPT. THINK ABOUT A MEMORY YOU TREASURE WITH SOMEONE WHO IS NO LONGER HERE.

💡 DAILY AFFIRMATIONS

1. ....

2. ....

3. ....

BONUS: *Read each affirmation 10x in the mirror & throughout the day for faster results.*

☀️ 3 PRIORITY GOALS

1. ....

2. ....

3. ....

💭 MY THOUGHTS & NOTES

Self-Care Check

○ **PHYSICAL**
Move or rest.

○ **SOCIAL**
Quality conversation.

○ **SPIRITUAL**
Good for the soul.

○ **HOUSEHOLD**
Cleaning or organizing.

○ **PAMPERING**
Treat yourself.

○ **PERSONAL**
Time on a hobby.

○ **EMOTIONAL**
Honor feelings.

○ **MENTAL**
Read or learn.

....

....

....

....

....

EVENING REFLECTIONS

Do not allow negative thoughts to enter your mind for they are the weeds that strangle confidence. —Bruce Lee

---

💗 GRATITUDE CHECK

TONIGHT I AM GRATEFUL FOR . . .

1. ....
2. ....
3. ....

Wellness Check

- ○ WORKOUT   ○ NATURE
- ○ MEDITATION   CAFFEINE: ....
- ○ NUTRITION   STEPS: ....

WATER INTAKE:

🧠 MENTAL HEALTH CHECK

RIGHT NOW I FEEL . . . (YOU MAY CHOOSE MORE THAN ONE)

- ○ HAPPY
- ○ LOVING
- ○ HOPEFUL
- ○ CALM
- ○ ANGRY
- ○ OVERWHELMED

- ○ PEACEFUL
- ○ CREATIVE
- ○ STRESSED
- ○ ANNOYED
- ○ POSITIVE
- ○ ANXIOUS

- ○ PROUD
- ○ SAD
- ○ TIRED
- ○ SCARED
- ○ JOYFUL
- ○ ....

SAY "I LOVE YOU" WITHOUT USING THOSE WORDS . . .

....
....
....

🏆 WINS FOR THE DAY

TODAY I ACCOMPLISHED . . .

....
....
....
....

💭 MY THOUGHTS & NOTES

....
....
....
....
....
....

Take life day by day, and be grateful for the little things. Don't get stressed over what you can't control.

I FEEL . . . 😄 😍 😐 😣 😔 😖   I WANT TO FEEL ....

🌱 GRATITUDE CHECK

TODAY I AM GRATEFUL FOR . . .

1. ....

2. ....

3. ....

SMILE OFTEN TODAY. IT TAKES LESS EFFORT THAN FROWNING, SLOWS YOUR HEART RATE, AND WILL RELEASE ENDORPHINS!

🔆 DAILY AFFIRMATIONS

1. ....

2. ....

3. ....

BONUS: *Read each affirmation 10x in the mirror & throughout the day for faster results.*

☆ 3 PRIORITY GOALS

1. ....

2. ....

3. ....

💭 MY THOUGHTS & NOTES

Self-Care Check

- ○ **PHYSICAL**
  Move or rest.
- ○ **SOCIAL**
  Quality conversation.
- ○ **SPIRITUAL**
  Good for the soul.
- ○ **HOUSEHOLD**
  Cleaning or organizing.
- ○ **PAMPERING**
  Treat yourself.
- ○ **PERSONAL**
  Time on a hobby.
- ○ **EMOTIONAL**
  Honor feelings.
- ○ **MENTAL**
  Read or learn.

....

....

....

....

....

Two things to remember in life. Take care of your thoughts when you are alone, and take care of your words when you are with people.

♡ GRATITUDE CHECK

TONIGHT I AM GRATEFUL FOR . . .

1. ....

2. ....

3. ....

Wellness Check

- ○ **WORKOUT**   ○ **NATURE**
- ○ **MEDITATION**   CAFFEINE: ....
- ○ **NUTRITION**   STEPS: ....

WATER INTAKE:

🥛 🥛 🥛 🥛 🥛 🥛 🥛

🧠 MENTAL HEALTH CHECK

RIGHT NOW I FEEL . . . (YOU MAY CHOOSE MORE THAN ONE)

○ HAPPY	○ PEACEFUL	○ PROUD
○ LOVING	○ CREATIVE	○ SAD
○ HOPEFUL	○ STRESSED	○ TIRED
○ CALM	○ ANNOYED	○ SCARED
○ ANGRY	○ POSITIVE	○ JOYFUL
○ OVERWHELMED	○ ANXIOUS	○ ....

AS YOU LOOK BACK, WHAT CONTINUES TO BE YOUR BIGGEST BLESSING?

....

....

....

🏆 WINS FOR THE DAY

TODAY I ACCOMPLISHED . . .

....

....

....

....

💭 MY THOUGHTS & NOTES

....

....

....

....

....

....

It's better to walk alone than with a crowd going in the wrong direction.

I FEEL . . . 😄 😍 😪 🙁 😟 😣   I WANT TO FEEL ....

🌱 GRATITUDE CHECK

TODAY I AM GRATEFUL FOR . . .

1. ....
2. ....
3. ....

PLAY! IT'S AMAZING WHAT HAPPENS WHEN YOU LET THE INNER CHILD OUT FOR SOME RECESS.

💡 DAILY AFFIRMATIONS

1. ....
2. ....
3. ....

BONUS: *Read each affirmation 10x in the mirror & throughout the day for faster results.*

☆ 3 PRIORITY GOALS

1. ....
2. ....
3. ....

💭 MY THOUGHTS & NOTES

Self-Care Check

○ **PHYSICAL**
Move or rest.

○ **SOCIAL**
Quality conversation.

○ **SPIRITUAL**
Good for the soul.

○ **HOUSEHOLD**
Cleaning or organizing.

○ **PAMPERING**
Treat yourself.

○ **PERSONAL**
Time on a hobby.

○ **EMOTIONAL**
Honor feelings.

○ **MENTAL**
Read or learn.

....
....
....
....
....

DATE: .... / .... / ....

You will never have to force anything that is meant to be.

🌹 GRATITUDE CHECK

TONIGHT I AM GRATEFUL FOR . . .

1. ....
2. ....
3. ....

Wellness Check

○ WORKOUT ○ NATURE
○ MEDITATION CAFFEINE: ....
○ NUTRITION STEPS: ....

WATER INTAKE:

🧠 MENTAL HEALTH CHECK

RIGHT NOW I FEEL . . . (YOU MAY CHOOSE MORE THAN ONE)

○ HAPPY	○ PEACEFUL	○ PROUD
○ LOVING	○ CREATIVE	○ SAD
○ HOPEFUL	○ STRESSED	○ TIRED
○ CALM	○ ANNOYED	○ SCARED
○ ANGRY	○ POSITIVE	○ JOYFUL
○ OVERWHELMED	○ ANXIOUS	○ ....

DESCRIBE YOUR SPIRITUAL OR RELIGIOUS BELIEFS . . .

....
....
....

🏆 WINS FOR THE DAY

TODAY I ACCOMPLISHED . . .

....
....
....
....

💭 MY THOUGHTS & NOTES

....
....
....
....
....

The most wasted of days is one without laughter. —e. e. cummings

I FEEL . . . 😃 😍 😔 🙁 😣 😖   I WANT TO FEEL ....

💟 GRATITUDE CHECK

TODAY I AM GRATEFUL FOR . . .

1. ....

2. ....

3. ....

**REPLACE APOLOGIES
WITH GRATITUDE.
ACKNOWLEDGE THE
GRACE OF OTHERS AND IT
WILL HELP YOU RELEASE
REGRET FROM YOURSELF.**

💡 DAILY AFFIRMATIONS

1. ....

2. ....

3. ....

BONUS: *Read each affirmation 10x in the mirror & throughout the day for faster results.*

☆ 3 PRIORITY GOALS

1. ....

2. ....

3. ....

Self-Care Check

○ **PHYSICAL**
Move or rest.

○ **SOCIAL**
Quality conversation.

○ **SPIRITUAL**
Good for the soul.

○ **HOUSEHOLD**
Cleaning or organizing.

○ **PAMPERING**
Treat yourself.

○ **PERSONAL**
Time on a hobby.

○ **EMOTIONAL**
Honor feelings.

○ **MENTAL**
Read or learn.

💭 MY THOUGHTS & NOTES

....

....

....

....

....

EVENING REFLECTIONS

Prayer can be the most powerful tool we have against worry, doubt, and fear.

💚 GRATITUDE CHECK

TONIGHT I AM GRATEFUL FOR . . .

1. ....

2. ....

3. ....

Wellness Check

○ WORKOUT   ○ NATURE

○ MEDITATION   CAFFEINE: ....

○ NUTRITION   STEPS: ....

WATER INTAKE:

🧠 MENTAL HEALTH CHECK

RIGHT NOW I FEEL . . . (YOU MAY CHOOSE MORE THAN ONE)

○ HAPPY	○ PEACEFUL	○ PROUD
○ LOVING	○ CREATIVE	○ SAD
○ HOPEFUL	○ STRESSED	○ TIRED
○ CALM	○ ANNOYED	○ SCARED
○ ANGRY	○ POSITIVE	○ JOYFUL
○ OVERWHELMED	○ ANXIOUS	○ ....

IF YOU COULD GIVE SOMEONE A PIECE OF ADVICE ABOUT LOVE, WHAT WOULD IT BE?

....

....

....

🏆 WINS FOR THE DAY

TODAY I ACCOMPLISHED . . .

....

....

....

....

💭 MY THOUGHTS & NOTES

....

....

....

....

....

Be happy right now, and not because everything is perfect, but because you choose to focus on each perfect, little moment.

I FEEL . . . 😄 😍 😴 ☹️ 😞 😣   I WANT TO FEEL ....

🫶 GRATITUDE CHECK

TODAY I AM GRATEFUL FOR . . .

1. ....
2. ....
3. ....

💡 DAILY AFFIRMATIONS

1. ....
2. ....
3. ....

BONUS: *Read each affirmation 10x in the mirror & throughout the day for faster results.*

IT'S HEALTHY TO LAUGH TODAY! LAUGHTER IS PROVEN TO INCREASE HAPPINESS AND SELF-ESTEEM, WHILE ALSO REDUCING NEGATIVE FEELINGS, SADNESS, AND STRESS.

☆ 3 PRIORITY GOALS

1. ....
2. ....
3. ....

💭 MY THOUGHTS & NOTES

Self-Care Check

- ○ **PHYSICAL**
  Move or rest.
- ○ **SOCIAL**
  Quality conversation.
- ○ **SPIRITUAL**
  Good for the soul.
- ○ **HOUSEHOLD**
  Cleaning or organizing.
- ○ **PAMPERING**
  Treat yourself.
- ○ **PERSONAL**
  Time on a hobby.
- ○ **EMOTIONAL**
  Honor feelings.
- ○ **MENTAL**
  Read or learn.

....
....
....
....
....

You cannot feel happiness if you don't appreciate what you already have.

🫀 GRATITUDE CHECK

TONIGHT I AM GRATEFUL FOR . . .

1. ....

2. ....

3. ....

Wellness Check

○ WORKOUT   ○ NATURE
○ MEDITATION   CAFFEINE: ....
○ NUTRITION   STEPS: ....

WATER INTAKE:

🧠 MENTAL HEALTH CHECK

RIGHT NOW I FEEL . . . (YOU MAY CHOOSE MORE THAN ONE)

○ HAPPY	○ PEACEFUL	○ PROUD
○ LOVING	○ CREATIVE	○ SAD
○ HOPEFUL	○ STRESSED	○ TIRED
○ CALM	○ ANNOYED	○ SCARED
○ ANGRY	○ POSITIVE	○ JOYFUL
○ OVERWHELMED	○ ANXIOUS	○ ....

DO YOU BELIEVE IN MIRACLES? IF SO, HAVE YOU EVER EXPERIENCED ONE?

....

....

....

🏆 WINS FOR THE DAY

TODAY I ACCOMPLISHED . . .

....

....

....

....

💭 MY THOUGHTS & NOTES

....

....

....

....

....

....

It is never too late to be what you might have been. —George Eliot

I FEEL . . . 😃 😍 😐 😦 😣 😖   I WANT TO FEEL ....

🫶 GRATITUDE CHECK

TODAY I AM GRATEFUL FOR . . .

1. ....
2. ....
3. ....

IT'S BEEN PROVEN THAT BOTH NEGATIVITY AND POSITIVITY ARE CONTAGIOUS. TAKE A LOOK AT THE PEOPLE YOU'RE SPENDING YOUR TIME WITH TODAY, AND PAY ATTENTION TO HOW YOU FEEL.

💡 DAILY AFFIRMATIONS

1. ....
2. ....
3. ....

BONUS: *Read each affirmation 10x in the mirror & throughout the day for faster results.*

✨ 3 PRIORITY GOALS

1. ....
2. ....
3. ....

Self-Care Check

- ○ **PHYSICAL**
  Move or rest.
- ○ **SOCIAL**
  Quality conversation.
- ○ **SPIRITUAL**
  Good for the soul.
- ○ **HOUSEHOLD**
  Cleaning or organizing.
- ○ **PAMPERING**
  Treat yourself.
- ○ **PERSONAL**
  Time on a hobby.
- ○ **EMOTIONAL**
  Honor feelings.
- ○ **MENTAL**
  Read or learn.

💭 MY THOUGHTS & NOTES

....
....
....
....
....

DATE: .... / .... / ....

Sometimes the key to happiness is letting a situation be what it is, instead of what you think it should be.

🧠 GRATITUDE CHECK

TONIGHT I AM GRATEFUL FOR . . .

1. ....

2. ....

3. ....

Wellness Check

○ **WORKOUT**   ○ **NATURE**

○ **MEDITATION** **CAFFEINE:** ....

○ **NUTRITION**   **STEPS:** ....

WATER INTAKE:

🧠 MENTAL HEALTH CHECK

RIGHT NOW I FEEL . . . (YOU MAY CHOOSE MORE THAN ONE)

○ HAPPY	○ PEACEFUL	○ PROUD
○ LOVING	○ CREATIVE	○ SAD
○ HOPEFUL	○ STRESSED	○ TIRED
○ CALM	○ ANNOYED	○ SCARED
○ ANGRY	○ POSITIVE	○ JOYFUL
○ OVERWHELMED	○ ANXIOUS	○ ....

WHAT LOVING THING DID YOU DO TODAY?

....

....

....

🏆 WINS FOR THE DAY

TODAY I ACCOMPLISHED . . .

....

....

....

....

....

💭 MY THOUGHTS & NOTES

....

....

....

....

....

....

Whoever is happy will make others happy too. —Anne Frank

___

I FEEL . . . 😀 😍 😴 ☹️ 😢 😣   I WANT TO FEEL ....

❤️ GRATITUDE CHECK

TODAY I AM GRATEFUL FOR . . .

1. ....

2. ....

3. ....

SCIENCE SAYS EVEN A SUBTLE CHANGE IN HOW YOU TALK TO YOURSELF CAN HELP YOU CONTROL YOUR FEELINGS, THOUGHTS, AND ACTIONS.

💡 DAILY AFFIRMATIONS

1. ....

2. ....

3. ....

BONUS: *Read each affirmation 10x in the mirror & throughout the day for faster results.*

☆ 3 PRIORITY GOALS

1. ....

2. ....

3. ....

Self-Care Check

○ **PHYSICAL**
Move or rest.

○ **SOCIAL**
Quality conversation.

○ **SPIRITUAL**
Good for the soul.

○ **HOUSEHOLD**
Cleaning or organizing.

○ **PAMPERING**
Treat yourself.

○ **PERSONAL**
Time on a hobby.

○ **EMOTIONAL**
Honor feelings.

○ **MENTAL**
Read or learn.

☁️ MY THOUGHTS & NOTES

....

....

....

....

....

Think positive thoughts. Say nice things. Do good for others.
Everything comes back.

GRATITUDE CHECK

TONIGHT I AM GRATEFUL FOR . . .

1. ....
2. ....
3. ....

Wellness Check

- ○ WORKOUT   ○ NATURE
- ○ MEDITATION CAFFEINE: ....
- ○ NUTRITION   STEPS: ....

WATER INTAKE:

MENTAL HEALTH CHECK

RIGHT NOW I FEEL . . . (YOU MAY CHOOSE MORE THAN ONE)

○ HAPPY	○ PEACEFUL	○ PROUD
○ LOVING	○ CREATIVE	○ SAD
○ HOPEFUL	○ STRESSED	○ TIRED
○ CALM	○ ANNOYED	○ SCARED
○ ANGRY	○ POSITIVE	○ JOYFUL
○ OVERWHELMED	○ ANXIOUS	○ ....

WHAT WERE THE HAPPIEST TIMES
OF YOUR CHILDHOOD?

....
....
....

🏆 WINS FOR THE DAY

TODAY I ACCOMPLISHED . . .

....
....
....

MY THOUGHTS & NOTES

....
....
....
....
....

Whatever you are, be a good one. —Abraham Lincoln

I FEEL . . . 😄 😍 😴 🙁 😣 😖   I WANT TO FEEL ....

🌹 GRATITUDE CHECK

TODAY I AM GRATEFUL FOR . . .

1. ....
2. ....
3. ....

HAPPY FEELINGS STEM FROM HAPPY THOUGHTS. TAKE TIME TO PAY ATTENTION TO HOW YOU FEEL, AND ONLY GIVE TIME TO WHAT MAKES YOU HAPPY.

💡 DAILY AFFIRMATIONS

1. ....
2. ....
3. ....

BONUS: *Read each affirmation 10x in the mirror & throughout the day for faster results.*

☀ 3 PRIORITY GOALS

1. ....
2. ....
3. ....

Self-Care Check

○ **PHYSICAL**
Move or rest.

○ **SOCIAL**
Quality conversation.

○ **SPIRITUAL**
Good for the soul.

○ **HOUSEHOLD**
Cleaning or organizing.

○ **PAMPERING**
Treat yourself.

○ **PERSONAL**
Time on a hobby.

○ **EMOTIONAL**
Honor feelings.

○ **MENTAL**
Read or learn.

☁ MY THOUGHTS & NOTES

....
....
....
....
....

Happiness begins from within. If you are not happy inside, the world around you will be full of things worth complaining about.

GRATITUDE CHECK

TONIGHT I AM GRATEFUL FOR . . .

1. ....
2. ....
3. ....

Wellness Check

○ WORKOUT   ○ NATURE
○ MEDITATION   CAFFEINE: ....
○ NUTRITION   STEPS: ....

WATER INTAKE:

MENTAL HEALTH CHECK

RIGHT NOW I FEEL . . . (YOU MAY CHOOSE MORE THAN ONE)

○ HAPPY	○ PEACEFUL	○ PROUD
○ LOVING	○ CREATIVE	○ SAD
○ HOPEFUL	○ STRESSED	○ TIRED
○ CALM	○ ANNOYED	○ SCARED
○ ANGRY	○ POSITIVE	○ JOYFUL
○ OVERWHELMED	○ ANXIOUS	○ ....

WHAT'S THE KEY TO A GREAT FRIENDSHIP?

....
....
....
....

WINS FOR THE DAY

TODAY I ACCOMPLISHED . . .

....
....
....
....

MY THOUGHTS & NOTES

....
....
....
....
....

It isn't where you came from. It's where you're going that counts.
—Ella Fitzgerald

I FEEL . . . 😃 😍 😴 🙁 😣 😖

I WANT TO FEEL ....

💗 GRATITUDE CHECK

TODAY I AM GRATEFUL FOR . . .

1. ....
2. ....
3. ....

**YOU HAVE CONTROL OVER
HOW YOU FEEL ABOUT
YOUR DAY. ASK YOURSELF,
"HOW CAN I MAKE TODAY
AMAZING?"**

🔆 DAILY AFFIRMATIONS

1. ....
2. ....
3. ....

BONUS: *Read each affirmation 10x in the mirror & throughout the day for faster results.*

☆ 3 PRIORITY GOALS

1. ....
2. ....
3. ....

☁ MY THOUGHTS & NOTES

Self-Care Check

- ○ **PHYSICAL**
  Move or rest.
- ○ **SOCIAL**
  Quality conversation.
- ○ **SPIRITUAL**
  Good for the soul.
- ○ **HOUSEHOLD**
  Cleaning or organizing.
- ○ **PAMPERING**
  Treat yourself.
- ○ **PERSONAL**
  Time on a hobby.
- ○ **EMOTIONAL**
  Honor feelings.
- ○ **MENTAL**
  Read or learn.

....
....
....
....
....

Be compassionate. Those who are not happy with themselves cannot possibly be happy with you.

GRATITUDE CHECK

TONIGHT I AM GRATEFUL FOR . . .

1. ....

2. ....

3. ....

Wellness Check

- ○ WORKOUT ○ NATURE
- ○ MEDITATION CAFFEINE: ....
- ○ NUTRITION STEPS: ....

WATER INTAKE:

MENTAL HEALTH CHECK

RIGHT NOW I FEEL . . . (YOU MAY CHOOSE MORE THAN ONE)

○ HAPPY	○ PEACEFUL	○ PROUD
○ LOVING	○ CREATIVE	○ SAD
○ HOPEFUL	○ STRESSED	○ TIRED
○ CALM	○ ANNOYED	○ SCARED
○ ANGRY	○ POSITIVE	○ JOYFUL
○ OVERWHELMED	○ ANXIOUS	○ ....

WHAT ARE FIVE THINGS YOU COULDN'T LIVE WITHOUT?

....

....

....

WINS FOR THE DAY

TODAY I ACCOMPLISHED . . .

....

....

....

MY THOUGHTS & NOTES

....

....

....

....

....

It's not what you look at that matters, it's what you see.
—Henry David Thoreau

I FEEL . . . 😄 😍 😴 🙁 😟 😣   I WANT TO FEEL ....

♡ GRATITUDE CHECK

TODAY I AM GRATEFUL FOR . . .

1. ....
2. ....
3. ....

**THINGS MAY NOT
ALWAYS GO AS PLANNED.
REMEMBER, THE BACKUP
PLAN CAN BE BETTER THAN
THE ORIGINAL.**

☀ DAILY AFFIRMATIONS

1. ....
2. ....
3. ....

BONUS: *Read each affirmation 10x in the mirror & throughout the day for faster results.*

☆ 3 PRIORITY GOALS

1. ....
2. ....
3. ....

☁ MY THOUGHTS & NOTES

Self-Care Check

○ **PHYSICAL**
Move or rest.

○ **SOCIAL**
Quality conversation.

○ **SPIRITUAL**
Good for the soul.

○ **HOUSEHOLD**
Cleaning or organizing.

○ **PAMPERING**
Treat yourself.

○ **PERSONAL**
Time on a hobby.

○ **EMOTIONAL**
Honor feelings.

○ **MENTAL**
Read or learn.

....
....
....
....
....

EVENING REFLECTIONS

Happiness can easily be found when you stop comparing your life with others' lives.

💗 GRATITUDE CHECK

TONIGHT I AM GRATEFUL FOR . . .

1. ....
2. ....
3. ....

Wellness Check

- ○ **WORKOUT**   ○ **NATURE**
- ○ **MEDITATION** **CAFFEINE:** ....
- ○ **NUTRITION**   **STEPS:** ....

WATER INTAKE:

🥛 🥛 🥛 🥛 🥛 🥛 🥛

🧠 MENTAL HEALTH CHECK

RIGHT NOW I FEEL . . . (YOU MAY CHOOSE MORE THAN ONE)

○ HAPPY	○ PEACEFUL	○ PROUD
○ LOVING	○ CREATIVE	○ SAD
○ HOPEFUL	○ STRESSED	○ TIRED
○ CALM	○ ANNOYED	○ SCARED
○ ANGRY	○ POSITIVE	○ JOYFUL
○ OVERWHELMED	○ ANXIOUS	○ ....

WHAT HABIT DO YOU WISH YOU COULD KEEP UP? TRY IT AGAIN TOMORROW!

....
....
....
....

🏆 WINS FOR THE DAY

TODAY I ACCOMPLISHED . . .

....
....
....
....
....

💭 MY THOUGHTS & NOTES

....
....
....
....
....
....

It's not whether you get knocked down; it's whether you get up.
—Vince Lombardi

I FEEL . . . 😃 😍 😒 🙁 ☹️ 😣   I WANT TO FEEL ....

❤️ GRATITUDE CHECK

TODAY I AM GRATEFUL FOR . . .

1. ....
2. ....
3. ....

**THINK OF 3 THINGS YOU
CAN DO TO BRING PEACE
INTO YOUR DAY . . . GO!**

💡 DAILY AFFIRMATIONS

1. ....
2. ....
3. ....

BONUS: *Read each affirmation 10x in the mirror & throughout the day for faster results.*

⭐ 3 PRIORITY GOALS

1. ....
2. ....
3. ....

Self-Care Check

○ **PHYSICAL**
Move or rest.

○ **SOCIAL**
Quality conversation.

○ **SPIRITUAL**
Good for the soul.

○ **HOUSEHOLD**
Cleaning or organizing.

○ **PAMPERING**
Treat yourself.

○ **PERSONAL**
Time on a hobby.

○ **EMOTIONAL**
Honor feelings.

○ **MENTAL**
Read or learn.

💭 MY THOUGHTS & NOTES

....
....
....
....

You may have a negative past, but that doesn't mean it has to be your future. Leave it behind you.

🫀 GRATITUDE CHECK

TONIGHT I AM GRATEFUL FOR . . .

1. ....
2. ....
3. ....

Wellness Check

○ **WORKOUT**   ○ **NATURE**
○ **MEDITATION**   **CAFFEINE:** ....
○ **NUTRITION**   **STEPS:** ....

WATER INTAKE:

🧠 MENTAL HEALTH CHECK

RIGHT NOW I FEEL . . . (YOU MAY CHOOSE MORE THAN ONE)

○ HAPPY	○ PEACEFUL	○ PROUD
○ LOVING	○ CREATIVE	○ SAD
○ HOPEFUL	○ STRESSED	○ TIRED
○ CALM	○ ANNOYED	○ SCARED
○ ANGRY	○ POSITIVE	○ JOYFUL
○ OVERWHELMED	○ ANXIOUS	○ ....

IS THERE ANYTHING YOU HAVE ALWAYS WANTED TO DO BUT HAVEN'T YET?

....
....
....

🏆 WINS FOR THE DAY

TODAY I ACCOMPLISHED . . .

....
....
....
....

💭 MY THOUGHTS & NOTES

....
....
....
....
....

If you want to live a happy life, tie it to a goal, not to people or things.
—Albert Einstein

I FEEL . . . 😄 😍 😴 🙁 😟 😖   I WANT TO FEEL ....

🫶 GRATITUDE CHECK

TODAY I AM GRATEFUL FOR . . .

1. ....

2. ....

3. ....

**HOLD FAST TO EVERY
KIND MESSAGE OR
E-MAIL YOU RECEIVE
TO BUILD A LIBRARY OF
ENCOURAGEMENT WHEN
YOU NEED IT.**

💡 DAILY AFFIRMATIONS

1. ....

2. ....

3. ....

BONUS: *Read each affirmation 10x in the mirror & throughout the day for faster results.*

☀ 3 PRIORITY GOALS

1. ....

2. ....

3. ....

Self-Care Check

○ **PHYSICAL**
Move or rest.

○ **SOCIAL**
Quality conversation.

○ **SPIRITUAL**
Good for the soul.

○ **HOUSEHOLD**
Cleaning or organizing.

○ **PAMPERING**
Treat yourself.

○ **PERSONAL**
Time on a hobby.

○ **EMOTIONAL**
Honor feelings.

○ **MENTAL**
Read or learn.

💭 MY THOUGHTS & NOTES

....

....

....

....

Change your thoughts, and you change your world.
—Norman Vincent Peale

♡ GRATITUDE CHECK

TONIGHT I AM GRATEFUL FOR . . .

1. ....

2. ....

3. ....

Wellness Check

○ WORKOUT ○ NATURE
○ MEDITATION CAFFEINE: ....
○ NUTRITION STEPS: ....

WATER INTAKE:

🧠 MENTAL HEALTH CHECK

RIGHT NOW I FEEL . . . (YOU MAY CHOOSE MORE THAN ONE)

○ HAPPY	○ PEACEFUL	○ PROUD
○ LOVING	○ CREATIVE	○ SAD
○ HOPEFUL	○ STRESSED	○ TIRED
○ CALM	○ ANNOYED	○ SCARED
○ ANGRY	○ POSITIVE	○ JOYFUL
○ OVERWHELMED	○ ANXIOUS	○ ....

LET'S TALK LEGACY . . .
WHAT DO YOU HOPE TO BE
REMEMBERED FOR?

....

....

....

🏆 WINS FOR THE DAY

TODAY I ACCOMPLISHED . . .

....

....

....

....

💭 MY THOUGHTS & NOTES

....

....

....

....

....

We overthink happiness.
Keep it simple. There is
something good in every
moment, find it and
keep your focus there.

@POSITIVEKRISTEN

30 Day Reflection

HAVE I FELT A BOOST OF HAPPINESS LATELY?   ✓   ✗

WHAT HAVE I LEARNED IN THE PAST 30 DAYS?

....
....
....
....

WHAT NEW HABITS HAVE I ACQUIRED?

....
....
....
....

WHAT CHALLENGES HAVE I HAD TO WORK ON?

....
....
....
....

WHAT ARE MY NEXT STEPS?

....
....
....
....

No matter how dark the moment, love and hope are always possible.
—George Chakiris

I FEEL . . . 😄 😍 😴 🙁 😟 😣   I WANT TO FEEL ....

❤️ GRATITUDE CHECK

TODAY I AM GRATEFUL FOR . . .

1. ....

2. ....

3. ....

**CHIN UP! A LITTLE
ADJUSTMENT IN YOUR
CHIN CAN ALTER HOW
YOU AND OTHERS
PERCEIVE YOU.**

💡 DAILY AFFIRMATIONS

1. ....

2. ....

3. ....

BONUS: *Read each affirmation 10x in the mirror & throughout the day for faster results.*

☀️ 3 PRIORITY GOALS

1. ....

2. ....

3. ....

💭 MY THOUGHTS & NOTES

Self-Care Check

○ **PHYSICAL**
Move or rest.

○ **SOCIAL**
Quality conversation.

○ **SPIRITUAL**
Good for the soul.

○ **HOUSEHOLD**
Cleaning or organizing.

○ **PAMPERING**
Treat yourself.

○ **PERSONAL**
Time on a hobby.

○ **EMOTIONAL**
Honor feelings.

○ **MENTAL**
Read or learn.

....
....
....
....
....

EVENING REFLECTIONS

Feeling gratitude and not expressing it is like wrapping a present and not giving it. —William Arthur Ward

🫀 GRATITUDE CHECK

TONIGHT I AM GRATEFUL FOR . . .

1. ....
2. ....
3. ....

Wellness Check

- ○ WORKOUT   ○ NATURE
- ○ MEDITATION   CAFFEINE: ....
- ○ NUTRITION   STEPS: ....

WATER INTAKE:

🧠 MENTAL HEALTH CHECK

RIGHT NOW I FEEL . . . (YOU MAY CHOOSE MORE THAN ONE)

○ HAPPY	○ PEACEFUL	○ PROUD
○ LOVING	○ CREATIVE	○ SAD
○ HOPEFUL	○ STRESSED	○ TIRED
○ CALM	○ ANNOYED	○ SCARED
○ ANGRY	○ POSITIVE	○ JOYFUL
○ OVERWHELMED	○ ANXIOUS	○ ....

WHAT DO YOU CONSIDER TO BE THE HAPPIEST MOMENT IN YOUR LIFETIME SO FAR?

....
....
....

🏆 WINS FOR THE DAY

TODAY I ACCOMPLISHED . . .

....
....
....
....

💭 MY THOUGHTS & NOTES

....
....
....
....
....

Never give up on a dream just because of the time it will take to accomplish it. The time will pass anyway. —Earl Nightingale

I FEEL . . . 😃 😍 😴 🙁 😟 😣   I WANT TO FEEL ....

🫶 GRATITUDE CHECK

TODAY I AM GRATEFUL FOR . . .

1. ....

2. ....

3. ....

FIND YOUR SACRED SPACE NO MATTER WHERE IT IS AND TAKE TIME TO BASK IN IT DAILY. YOU'LL BE HAPPIER FOR IT.

💡 DAILY AFFIRMATIONS

1. ....

2. ....

3. ....

BONUS: *Read each affirmation 10x in the mirror & throughout the day for faster results.*

☀ 3 PRIORITY GOALS

1. ....

2. ....

3. ....

💭 MY THOUGHTS & NOTES

Self-Care Check

○ **PHYSICAL**
Move or rest.

○ **SOCIAL**
Quality conversation.

○ **SPIRITUAL**
Good for the soul.

○ **HOUSEHOLD**
Cleaning or organizing.

○ **PAMPERING**
Treat yourself.

○ **PERSONAL**
Time on a hobby.

○ **EMOTIONAL**
Honor feelings.

○ **MENTAL**
Read or learn.

....

....

....

....

....

It's not the load that breaks you down, it's the way you carry it.
—Lou Holtz

🌀 GRATITUDE CHECK

TONIGHT I AM GRATEFUL FOR . . .

1. ....

2. ....

3. ....

Wellness Check

- ○ **WORKOUT**   ○ **NATURE**
- ○ **MEDITATION**   **CAFFEINE:** ....
- ○ **NUTRITION**   **STEPS:** ....

WATER INTAKE:

🥛 🥛 🥛 🥛 🥛 🥛 🥛 🥛

🧠 MENTAL HEALTH CHECK

RIGHT NOW I FEEL . . . (YOU MAY CHOOSE MORE THAN ONE)

○ HAPPY	○ PEACEFUL	○ PROUD
○ LOVING	○ CREATIVE	○ SAD
○ HOPEFUL	○ STRESSED	○ TIRED
○ CALM	○ ANNOYED	○ SCARED
○ ANGRY	○ POSITIVE	○ JOYFUL
○ OVERWHELMED	○ ANXIOUS	○ ....

HOW DID YOU HELP SOMEONE
ELSE TODAY?

....

....

....

🏆 WINS FOR THE DAY

TODAY I ACCOMPLISHED . . .

....

....

....

....

💭 MY THOUGHTS & NOTES

....

....

....

....

....

Never give up, for that is just the place and time that the tide will turn. —Harriet Beecher Stowe

I FEEL . . . 😄 😍 😴 🙁 😣 😖   I WANT TO FEEL ....

🥬 GRATITUDE CHECK

TODAY I AM GRATEFUL FOR . . .

1. ....
2. ....
3. ....

MAKE A SMALL ACHIEVABLE BUCKET LIST TODAY. EVEN IF IT'S TRYING A NEW RECIPE, GIVE YOURSELF THE ENDORPHINS YOU DESERVE.

💡 DAILY AFFIRMATIONS

1. ....
2. ....
3. ....

BONUS: *Read each affirmation 10x in the mirror & throughout the day for faster results.*

☀ 3 PRIORITY GOALS

1. ....
2. ....
3. ....

Self-Care Check

○ **PHYSICAL**
Move or rest.

○ **SOCIAL**
Quality conversation.

○ **SPIRITUAL**
Good for the soul.

○ **HOUSEHOLD**
Cleaning or organizing.

○ **PAMPERING**
Treat yourself.

○ **PERSONAL**
Time on a hobby.

○ **EMOTIONAL**
Honor feelings.

○ **MENTAL**
Read or learn.

☁ MY THOUGHTS & NOTES

....
....
....
....
....

EVENING REFLECTIONS

DATE: .... /........... / ....

Life has no limitations, except the ones you make. —Les Brown

GRATITUDE CHECK

TONIGHT I AM GRATEFUL FOR . . .

1. ....

2. ....

3. ....

Wellness Check

- O **WORKOUT**
- O **NATURE**
- O **MEDITATION**
- **CAFFEINE:** ....
- O **NUTRITION**
- **STEPS:** ....

WATER INTAKE:

MENTAL HEALTH CHECK

RIGHT NOW I FEEL . . . (YOU MAY CHOOSE MORE THAN ONE)

O **HAPPY**	O **PEACEFUL**	O **PROUD**
O **LOVING**	O **CREATIVE**	O **SAD**
O **HOPEFUL**	O **STRESSED**	O **TIRED**
O **CALM**	O **ANNOYED**	O **SCARED**
O **ANGRY**	O **POSITIVE**	O **JOYFUL**
O **OVERWHELMED**	O **ANXIOUS**	O ....

WHAT ABOUT TODAY MADE YOU SMILE?

....

....

....

WINS FOR THE DAY

TODAY I ACCOMPLISHED . . .

....

....

....

....

MY THOUGHTS & NOTES

....

....

....

....

....

When you focus on the good, the good gets better.

I FEEL . . . 😄 😍 😴 🙁 😟 😣   I WANT TO FEEL ....

❤️ GRATITUDE CHECK

TODAY I AM GRATEFUL FOR . . .

1. ....

2. ....

3. ....

SPEND MONEY ON SMALL PLEASURES THAT MAKE YOU HAPPY. PAMPER YOURSELF WITHOUT FEELING GUILTY.

💡 DAILY AFFIRMATIONS

1. ....

2. ....

3. ....

BONUS: *Read each affirmation 10x in the mirror & throughout the day for faster results.*

☀️ 3 PRIORITY GOALS

1. ....

2. ....

3. ....

Self-Care Check

○ **PHYSICAL**
Move or rest.

○ **SOCIAL**
Quality conversation.

○ **SPIRITUAL**
Good for the soul.

○ **HOUSEHOLD**
Cleaning or organizing.

○ **PAMPERING**
Treat yourself.

○ **PERSONAL**
Time on a hobby.

○ **EMOTIONAL**
Honor feelings.

○ **MENTAL**
Read or learn.

☁️ MY THOUGHTS & NOTES

....

....

....

....

....

When we are happy, we glow from the inside out. We see the beauty of life and allow for more opportunities to be possible.

❤ GRATITUDE CHECK

TONIGHT I AM GRATEFUL FOR . . .

1. ....

2. ....

3. ....

Wellness Check

○ WORKOUT   ○ NATURE
○ MEDITATION CAFFEINE: ....
○ NUTRITION   STEPS: ....

WATER INTAKE:

🧠 MENTAL HEALTH CHECK

RIGHT NOW I FEEL . . . (YOU MAY CHOOSE MORE THAN ONE)

○ HAPPY   ○ PEACEFUL   ○ PROUD
○ LOVING   ○ CREATIVE   ○ SAD
○ HOPEFUL   ○ STRESSED   ○ TIRED
○ CALM   ○ ANNOYED   ○ SCARED
○ ANGRY   ○ POSITIVE   ○ JOYFUL
○ OVERWHELMED   ○ ANXIOUS   ○ ....

EVENING GRATITUDE CHECK!
3 THINGS YOU ARE MOST
THANKFUL FOR . . .

....

....

....

🏆 WINS FOR THE DAY

TODAY I ACCOMPLISHED . . .

....

....

....

....

💭 MY THOUGHTS & NOTES

....

....

....

....

....

Don't wait. The time will never be just right. —Napoleon Hill

I FEEL . . . 😃 😍 😑💤 🙁 😣 😖   I WANT TO FEEL ....

♡ GRATITUDE CHECK

TODAY I AM GRATEFUL FOR . . .

1. ....

2. ....

3. ....

GET A NEW PLANT OR FLOWER. STUDIES SHOW THEY CAN HELP YOU FOCUS, IMPROVE YOUR MOOD, CLEAN THE AIR, AND REDUCE STRESS.

💡 DAILY AFFIRMATIONS

1. ....

2. ....

3. ....

BONUS: *Read each affirmation 10x in the mirror & throughout the day for faster results.*

☀ 3 PRIORITY GOALS

1. ....

2. ....

3. ....

Self-Care Check

○ **PHYSICAL**
Move or rest.

○ **SOCIAL**
Quality conversation.

○ **SPIRITUAL**
Good for the soul.

○ **HOUSEHOLD**
Cleaning or organizing.

○ **PAMPERING**
Treat yourself.

○ **PERSONAL**
Time on a hobby.

○ **EMOTIONAL**
Honor feelings.

○ **MENTAL**
Read or learn.

💭 MY THOUGHTS & NOTES

....

....

....

....

....

EVENING REFLECTIONS

The best way to predict the future is to create it. —Abraham Lincoln

---

GRATITUDE CHECK

TONIGHT I AM GRATEFUL FOR . . .

1. ....

2. ....

3. ....

Wellness Check

○ WORKOUT   ○ NATURE

○ MEDITATION   CAFFEINE: ....

○ NUTRITION   STEPS: ....

WATER INTAKE:

MENTAL HEALTH CHECK

RIGHT NOW I FEEL . . . (YOU MAY CHOOSE MORE THAN ONE)

○ HAPPY	○ PEACEFUL	○ PROUD
○ LOVING	○ CREATIVE	○ SAD
○ HOPEFUL	○ STRESSED	○ TIRED
○ CALM	○ ANNOYED	○ SCARED
○ ANGRY	○ POSITIVE	○ JOYFUL
○ OVERWHELMED	○ ANXIOUS	○ ....

WHO ARE YOUR MENTORS? WHY?

....

....

....

WINS FOR THE DAY

TODAY I ACCOMPLISHED . . .

....

....

....

....

MY THOUGHTS & NOTES

....

....

....

....

....

How you think about a problem is more important than the problem itself. So always think positively. —Norman Vincent Peale

I FEEL . . . 😄 😍 😐 😞 😟 😣   I WANT TO FEEL ....

♡ GRATITUDE CHECK

TODAY I AM GRATEFUL FOR . . .

1. ....

2. ....

3. ....

SNUGGLE UP WITH A GOOD BOOK. BOOKS TAKE OUR IMAGINATIONS TO OTHER WORLDS AND ARE BACKED BY SCIENCE TO IMPROVE MENTAL HEALTH.

💡 DAILY AFFIRMATIONS

1. ....

2. ....

3. ....

BONUS: *Read each affirmation 10x in the mirror & throughout the day for faster results.*

☀ 3 PRIORITY GOALS

1. ....

2. ....

3. ....

Self-Care Check

- O **PHYSICAL**
  Move or rest.
- O **SOCIAL**
  Quality conversation.
- O **SPIRITUAL**
  Good for the soul.
- O **HOUSEHOLD**
  Cleaning or organizing.
- O **PAMPERING**
  Treat yourself.
- O **PERSONAL**
  Time on a hobby.
- O **EMOTIONAL**
  Honor feelings.
- O **MENTAL**
  Read or learn.

☁ MY THOUGHTS & NOTES

....

....

....

....

....

Once you choose hope, anything's possible. —Christopher Reeve

---

🧠 GRATITUDE CHECK

TONIGHT I AM GRATEFUL FOR . . .

1. ....
2. ....
3. ....

Wellness Check

- ○ **WORKOUT**   ○ **NATURE**
- ○ **MEDITATION**   CAFFEINE: ....
- ○ **NUTRITION**   STEPS: ....

WATER INTAKE:

🥛 🥛 🥛 🥛 🥛 🥛 🥛

🧠 MENTAL HEALTH CHECK

RIGHT NOW I FEEL . . . (YOU MAY CHOOSE MORE THAN ONE)

○ HAPPY	○ PEACEFUL	○ PROUD
○ LOVING	○ CREATIVE	○ SAD
○ HOPEFUL	○ STRESSED	○ TIRED
○ CALM	○ ANNOYED	○ SCARED
○ ANGRY	○ POSITIVE	○ JOYFUL
○ OVERWHELMED	○ ANXIOUS	○ ....

WHERE IS YOUR "HAPPY PLACE"?
DESCRIBE IT.

....
....
....
....

🏆 WINS FOR THE DAY

TODAY I ACCOMPLISHED . . .

....
....
....
....

💭 MY THOUGHTS & NOTES

....
....
....
....
....

All you need is the plan, the road map, and the courage to press on to your destination. —Earl Nightingale

---

I FEEL . . . 😃 😍 😴 🙁 😣 😖   I WANT TO FEEL ....

❤ GRATITUDE CHECK

TODAY I AM GRATEFUL FOR . . .

1. ....

2. ....

3. ....

SPEND TIME WITH KIND PEOPLE. IF YOU CAN'T FIND A KIND PERSON, BE ONE FOR SOMEONE ELSE.

💡 DAILY AFFIRMATIONS

1. ....

2. ....

3. ....

BONUS: *Read each affirmation 10x in the mirror & throughout the day for faster results.*

☀ 3 PRIORITY GOALS

1. ....

2. ....

3. ....

💭 MY THOUGHTS & NOTES

Self-Care Check

○ **PHYSICAL**
Move or rest.

○ **SOCIAL**
Quality conversation.

○ **SPIRITUAL**
Good for the soul.

○ **HOUSEHOLD**
Cleaning or organizing.

○ **PAMPERING**
Treat yourself.

○ **PERSONAL**
Time on a hobby.

○ **EMOTIONAL**
Honor feelings.

○ **MENTAL**
Read or learn.

....

....

....

....

....

The only person you are destined to become is the person you decide to be. —Ralph Waldo Emerson

GRATITUDE CHECK

TONIGHT I AM GRATEFUL FOR . . .

1. ....

2. ....

3. ....

MENTAL HEALTH CHECK

RIGHT NOW I FEEL . . . (YOU MAY CHOOSE MORE THAN ONE)

- ○ HAPPY
- ○ LOVING
- ○ HOPEFUL
- ○ CALM
- ○ ANGRY
- ○ OVERWHELMED
- ○ PEACEFUL
- ○ CREATIVE
- ○ STRESSED
- ○ ANNOYED
- ○ POSITIVE
- ○ ANXIOUS
- ○ PROUD
- ○ SAD
- ○ TIRED
- ○ SCARED
- ○ JOYFUL
- ○ ....

Wellness Check

- ○ WORKOUT   ○ NATURE
- ○ MEDITATION   CAFFEINE: ....
- ○ NUTRITION   STEPS: ....

WATER INTAKE:

WHAT'S YOUR PASSION, AND HOW DID YOU DISCOVER IT?

....

....

....

WINS FOR THE DAY

TODAY I ACCOMPLISHED . . .

....

....

....

....

MY THOUGHTS & NOTES

....

....

....

....

....

Show me someone who has done something worthwhile, and I'll show you someone who has overcome adversity. —Lou Holtz

I FEEL . . . 😆 😍 😔 🙁 😢 😣   I WANT TO FEEL ....

🫶 GRATITUDE CHECK

TODAY I AM GRATEFUL FOR . . .

1. ....

2. ....

3. ....

**BE GENEROUS TODAY—
WHETHER THAT MEANS
GIVING A GOOD TIP OR
VOLUNTEERING YOUR
TIME FOR A CAUSE.**

💡 DAILY AFFIRMATIONS

1. ....

2. ....

3. ....

BONUS: *Read each affirmation 10x in the mirror & throughout the day for faster results.*

☀ 3 PRIORITY GOALS

1. ....

2. ....

3. ....

Self-Care Check

○ **PHYSICAL**
Move or rest.

○ **SOCIAL**
Quality conversation.

○ **SPIRITUAL**
Good for the soul.

○ **HOUSEHOLD**
Cleaning or organizing.

○ **PAMPERING**
Treat yourself.

○ **PERSONAL**
Time on a hobby.

○ **EMOTIONAL**
Honor feelings.

○ **MENTAL**
Read or learn.

💭 MY THOUGHTS & NOTES

....

....

....

....

....

The sun himself is weak when he first rises, and gathers strength and courage as the day gets on. —Charles Dickens

🫶 GRATITUDE CHECK

TONIGHT I AM GRATEFUL FOR . . .

1. ....

2. ....

3. ....

🧠 MENTAL HEALTH CHECK

RIGHT NOW I FEEL . . . (YOU MAY CHOOSE MORE THAN ONE)

○ HAPPY	○ PEACEFUL	○ PROUD
○ LOVING	○ CREATIVE	○ SAD
○ HOPEFUL	○ STRESSED	○ TIRED
○ CALM	○ ANNOYED	○ SCARED
○ ANGRY	○ POSITIVE	○ JOYFUL
○ OVERWHELMED	○ ANXIOUS	○ ....

Wellness Check

○ WORKOUT   ○ NATURE
○ MEDITATION   CAFFEINE: ....
○ NUTRITION   STEPS: ....

WATER INTAKE:

IF YOU KNEW YOU COULDN'T FAIL, WHAT WOULD YOU DO?

....

....

....

🏆 WINS FOR THE DAY

TODAY I ACCOMPLISHED . . .

....

....

....

....

💭 MY THOUGHTS & NOTES

....

....

....

....

....

Oh yes, the past can hurt. But you can either run from it, or learn from it. —Rafiki, *The Lion King*

I FEEL ... 😄 😍 😴 😦 😟 😣   I WANT TO FEEL ....

🫶 GRATITUDE CHECK

TODAY I AM GRATEFUL FOR ...

1. ....

2. ....

3. ....

**WHAT PARTS OF YOUR
LIFE DO YOU LOVE SO
MUCH THAT IT ALREADY
FEELS LIKE YOU WON
THE LOTTERY?**

💡 DAILY AFFIRMATIONS

1. ....

2. ....

3. ....

BONUS: *Read each affirmation 10x in the mirror & throughout the day for faster results.*

☆ 3 PRIORITY GOALS

1. ....

2. ....

3. ....

Self-Care Check

○ **PHYSICAL**   ○ **SOCIAL**
Move or rest.   Quality conversation.

○ **SPIRITUAL**   ○ **HOUSEHOLD**
Good for the soul.   Cleaning or organizing.

○ **PAMPERING**   ○ **PERSONAL**
Treat yourself.   Time on a hobby.

○ **EMOTIONAL**   ○ **MENTAL**
Honor feelings.   Read or learn.

💭 MY THOUGHTS & NOTES

....

....

....

....

....

Always be a first-rate version of yourself, instead of a second-rate version of somebody else. —Judy Garland

---

💚 GRATITUDE CHECK

TONIGHT I AM GRATEFUL FOR . . .

1. ....

2. ....

3. ....

Wellness Check

○ WORKOUT　　○ NATURE
○ MEDITATION　CAFFEINE: ....
○ NUTRITION　　STEPS: ....

WATER INTAKE:

🥛 🥛 🥛 🥛 🥛 🥛 🥛

🧠 MENTAL HEALTH CHECK

RIGHT NOW I FEEL . . . (YOU MAY CHOOSE MORE THAN ONE)

○ HAPPY　　　　○ PEACEFUL　　○ PROUD
○ LOVING　　　 ○ CREATIVE　　○ SAD
○ HOPEFUL　　　○ STRESSED　　○ TIRED
○ CALM　　　　 ○ ANNOYED　　 ○ SCARED
○ ANGRY　　　　○ POSITIVE　　 ○ JOYFUL
○ OVERWHELMED　○ ANXIOUS　　 ○ ....

WHAT CAN YOU DO TO BRING MORE JOY INTO YOUR DAY TOMORROW?

....
....
....

🏆 WINS FOR THE DAY

TODAY I ACCOMPLISHED . . .

....
....
....
....

💭 MY THOUGHTS & NOTES

....
....
....
....
....
....

Life's like a movie, write your own ending. Keep believing, keep pretending. —Jim Hensen

---

I FEEL . . . 😄 😍 😑 🙁 😟 😣   I WANT TO FEEL ....

♡ GRATITUDE CHECK

TODAY I AM GRATEFUL FOR . . .

1. ....

2. ....

3. ....

DON'T BE SCARED TO ASK FOR HELP WHEN YOU NEED IT. WE ALL NEED SOMEBODY TO LEAN ON.

💡 DAILY AFFIRMATIONS

1. ....

2. ....

3. ....

BONUS: *Read each affirmation 10x in the mirror & throughout the day for faster results.*

☀ 3 PRIORITY GOALS

1. ....

2. ....

3. ....

Self-Care Check

○ **PHYSICAL**
Move or rest.

○ **SOCIAL**
Quality conversation.

○ **SPIRITUAL**
Good for the soul.

○ **HOUSEHOLD**
Cleaning or organizing.

○ **PAMPERING**
Treat yourself.

○ **PERSONAL**
Time on a hobby.

○ **EMOTIONAL**
Honor feelings.

○ **MENTAL**
Read or learn.

☁ MY THOUGHTS & NOTES

....

....

....

....

....

Learning never exhausts the mind. —Leonardo Da Vinci

❤ GRATITUDE CHECK

TONIGHT I AM GRATEFUL FOR . . .

1. ....

2. ....

3. ....

Wellness Check

○ WORKOUT   ○ NATURE
○ MEDITATION CAFFEINE: ....
○ NUTRITION   STEPS: ....

WATER INTAKE:

🧠 MENTAL HEALTH CHECK

RIGHT NOW I FEEL . . . (YOU MAY CHOOSE MORE THAN ONE)

○ HAPPY	○ PEACEFUL	○ PROUD
○ LOVING	○ CREATIVE	○ SAD
○ HOPEFUL	○ STRESSED	○ TIRED
○ CALM	○ ANNOYED	○ SCARED
○ ANGRY	○ POSITIVE	○ JOYFUL
○ OVERWHELMED	○ ANXIOUS	○ ....

WHAT DO YOU WISH YOU WERE
DOING MORE OF?

....

....

....

🏆 WINS FOR THE DAY

TODAY I ACCOMPLISHED . . .

....

....

....

☁ MY THOUGHTS & NOTES

....

....

....

....

....

Strength shows not only in the ability to persist, but in the ability to start over. —F. Scott Fitzgerald

---

I FEEL . . . 😃 😎 😔 🙁 😢 😣   I WANT TO FEEL ....

❤ GRATITUDE CHECK

TODAY I AM GRATEFUL FOR . . .

1. ....

2. ....

3. ....

WAKE UP TO SOMETHING CALM. CHANGE YOUR ALARM TO SOMETHING SOOTHING TO WAKE UP FEELING MORE PEACEFUL OR REMAIN QUIET FOR AT LEAST 5 MINUTES AFTER WAKING.

💡 DAILY AFFIRMATIONS

1. ....

2. ....

3. ....

BONUS: *Read each affirmation 10x in the mirror & throughout the day for faster results.*

☀ 3 PRIORITY GOALS

1. ....

2. ....

3. ....

Self-Care Check

○ **PHYSICAL**
Move or rest.

○ **SOCIAL**
Quality conversation.

○ **SPIRITUAL**
Good for the soul.

○ **HOUSEHOLD**
Cleaning or organizing.

○ **PAMPERING**
Treat yourself.

○ **PERSONAL**
Time on a hobby.

○ **EMOTIONAL**
Honor feelings.

○ **MENTAL**
Read or learn.

☁ MY THOUGHTS & NOTES

....

....

....

....

....

You create your thoughts, emotions, and actions.
Create them intentionally.

GRATITUDE CHECK

TONIGHT I AM GRATEFUL FOR . . .

1. ....

2. ....

3. ....

Wellness Check

- ○ WORKOUT   ○ NATURE
- ○ MEDITATION   CAFFEINE: ....
- ○ NUTRITION   STEPS: ....

WATER INTAKE:

MENTAL HEALTH CHECK

RIGHT NOW I FEEL . . . (YOU MAY CHOOSE MORE THAN ONE)

○ HAPPY	○ PEACEFUL	○ PROUD
○ LOVING	○ CREATIVE	○ SAD
○ HOPEFUL	○ STRESSED	○ TIRED
○ CALM	○ ANNOYED	○ SCARED
○ ANGRY	○ POSITIVE	○ JOYFUL
○ OVERWHELMED	○ ANXIOUS	○ ....

WHAT'S THE MOST IMPORTANT
THING TO FOCUS ON THIS WEEK?

....

....

....

WINS FOR THE DAY

TODAY I ACCOMPLISHED . . .

....

....

....

MY THOUGHTS & NOTES

....

....

....

....

....

DATE: .... / .... / ....

Look at life with the eyes of a child. —Henri Matisse

I FEEL . . . 😃 😍 😑 🙁 😣 😫   I WANT TO FEEL ....

🌹 GRATITUDE CHECK

TODAY I AM GRATEFUL FOR . . .

1. ....
2. ....
3. ....

BE MINDFUL OF YOUR THOUGHTS AND SELF-TALK WHENEVER POSSIBLE. RECOGNIZE WHENEVER YOU CATCH YOURSELF IN A LIMITING OR NEGATIVE MINDSET, AND LET IT GO.

💡 DAILY AFFIRMATIONS

1. ....
2. ....
3. ....

BONUS: *Read each affirmation 10x in the mirror & throughout the day for faster results.*

☼ 3 PRIORITY GOALS

1. ....
2. ....
3. ....

☁ MY THOUGHTS & NOTES

Self-Care Check

○ **PHYSICAL**
Move or rest.

○ **SOCIAL**
Quality conversation.

○ **SPIRITUAL**
Good for the soul.

○ **HOUSEHOLD**
Cleaning or organizing.

○ **PAMPERING**
Treat yourself.

○ **PERSONAL**
Time on a hobby.

○ **EMOTIONAL**
Honor feelings.

○ **MENTAL**
Read or learn.

....
....
....
....
....

EVENING REFLECTIONS

Be the person you needed when you were going through hard times.

💗 GRATITUDE CHECK

TONIGHT I AM GRATEFUL FOR . . .

1. ....

2. ....

3. ....

Wellness Check

○ WORKOUT   ○ NATURE

○ MEDITATION CAFFEINE: ....

○ NUTRITION STEPS: ....

WATER INTAKE:

🧠 MENTAL HEALTH CHECK

RIGHT NOW I FEEL . . . (YOU MAY CHOOSE MORE THAN ONE)

○ HAPPY	○ PEACEFUL	○ PROUD
○ LOVING	○ CREATIVE	○ SAD
○ HOPEFUL	○ STRESSED	○ TIRED
○ CALM	○ ANNOYED	○ SCARED
○ ANGRY	○ POSITIVE	○ JOYFUL
○ OVERWHELMED	○ ANXIOUS	○ ....

WRITE ABOUT A MISTAKE
THAT TURNED OUT TO BE A
BLESSING . . .

....

....

....

🏆 WINS FOR THE DAY

TODAY I ACCOMPLISHED . . .

....

....

....

....

💭 MY THOUGHTS & NOTES

....

....

....

....

....

Train your mind to be grateful, think positively, and manifest what you want. —Lewis Howes

I FEEL . . . 😄 😍 😴 🙁 😣 😖   I WANT TO FEEL ....

🫶 GRATITUDE CHECK

TODAY I AM GRATEFUL FOR . . .

1. ....
2. ....
3. ....

TRY TO STAY MINDFUL OF WHERE YOU ARE, WHAT YOU'RE THINKING, AND WHAT YOU ARE DOING. USE THIS EXERCISE WHENEVER YOU NEED TO UNWIND AND ATTRACT POSITIVE ENERGY.

💡 DAILY AFFIRMATIONS

1. ....
2. ....
3. ....

BONUS: *Read each affirmation 10x in the mirror & throughout the day for faster results.*

☼ 3 PRIORITY GOALS

1. ....
2. ....
3. ....

☁ MY THOUGHTS & NOTES

Self-Care Check

○ **PHYSICAL**
Move or rest.

○ **SOCIAL**
Quality conversation.

○ **SPIRITUAL**
Good for the soul.

○ **HOUSEHOLD**
Cleaning or organizing.

○ **PAMPERING**
Treat yourself.

○ **PERSONAL**
Time on a hobby.

○ **EMOTIONAL**
Honor feelings.

○ **MENTAL**
Read or learn.

....
....
....
....
....

EVENING REFLECTIONS

Protect your peace. Cherish moments of joy. Live in love.

GRATITUDE CHECK

TONIGHT I AM GRATEFUL FOR . . .

1. ....

2. ....

3. ....

Wellness Check

○ **WORKOUT**   ○ **NATURE**

○ **MEDITATION**   CAFFEINE: ....

○ **NUTRITION**   STEPS: ....

WATER INTAKE:

MENTAL HEALTH CHECK

RIGHT NOW I FEEL . . . (YOU MAY CHOOSE MORE THAN ONE)

○ **HAPPY**	○ **PEACEFUL**	○ **PROUD**
○ **LOVING**	○ **CREATIVE**	○ **SAD**
○ **HOPEFUL**	○ **STRESSED**	○ **TIRED**
○ **CALM**	○ **ANNOYED**	○ **SCARED**
○ **ANGRY**	○ **POSITIVE**	○ **JOYFUL**
○ **OVERWHELMED**	○ **ANXIOUS**	○ ....

WHAT GIVES YOU HOPE? WHY?

....

....

....

WINS FOR THE DAY

TODAY I ACCOMPLISHED . . .

....

....

....

....

MY THOUGHTS & NOTES

....

....

....

....

....

It's the everyday little things . . . like a cozy blanket, a good book, and being surrounded by those I love.

I FEEL . . . 😄 😍 😴 🙁 😢 😖   I WANT TO FEEL ....

🫶 GRATITUDE CHECK

TODAY I AM GRATEFUL FOR . . .

1. ....

2. ....

3. ....

STOP SEEKING APPROVAL FROM OTHERS. YOU ARE ENOUGH AS YOU ARE; YOU DON'T NEED TO PROVE ANYTHING TO ANYONE. LIVE UP TO YOUR OWN EXPECTATIONS.

💡 DAILY AFFIRMATIONS

1. ....

2. ....

3. ....

BONUS: *Read each affirmation 10x in the mirror & throughout the day for faster results.*

☆ 3 PRIORITY GOALS

1. ....

2. ....

3. ....

Self-Care Check

- ○ **PHYSICAL** Move or rest.
- ○ **SOCIAL** Quality conversation.
- ○ **SPIRITUAL** Good for the soul.
- ○ **HOUSEHOLD** Cleaning or organizing.
- ○ **PAMPERING** Treat yourself.
- ○ **PERSONAL** Time on a hobby.
- ○ **EMOTIONAL** Honor feelings.
- ○ **MENTAL** Read or learn.

💭 MY THOUGHTS & NOTES

....

....

....

....

....

Life only becomes too hard when you stop believing. Keep your head up and stay positive.

♡ GRATITUDE CHECK

TONIGHT I AM GRATEFUL FOR . . .

1. ....

2. ....

3. ....

Wellness Check

○ WORKOUT   ○ NATURE
○ MEDITATION   CAFFEINE: ....
○ NUTRITION   STEPS: ....

WATER INTAKE:

🧠 MENTAL HEALTH CHECK

RIGHT NOW I FEEL . . . (YOU MAY CHOOSE MORE THAN ONE)

○ HAPPY	○ PEACEFUL	○ PROUD
○ LOVING	○ CREATIVE	○ SAD
○ HOPEFUL	○ STRESSED	○ TIRED
○ CALM	○ ANNOYED	○ SCARED
○ ANGRY	○ POSITIVE	○ JOYFUL
○ OVERWHELMED	○ ANXIOUS	○

WHAT CAN YOU DO FOR YOURSELF THAT WOULD FEEL EXTRA SPECIAL?

....

....

....

🏆 WINS FOR THE DAY

TODAY I ACCOMPLISHED . . .

....

....

....

....

💭 MY THOUGHTS & NOTES

....

....

....

....

....

DATE: .... / .... / ....

Your big opportunity may be right where you are now.
—Napoleon Hill

I FEEL . . . 😄 😍 😴 😟 😢 😣   I WANT TO FEEL ....

❤️ GRATITUDE CHECK

TODAY I AM GRATEFUL FOR . . .

1. ....
2. ....
3. ....

CONSIDER HOW YOUR FOOD MAKES YOU FEEL TODAY. EAT WHAT MAKES YOU FEEL YOUR BEST AND AVOID FOODS THAT MAKE YOU FEEL SLUGGISH.

💡 DAILY AFFIRMATIONS

1. ....
2. ....
3. ....

BONUS: Read each affirmation 10x in the mirror & throughout the day for faster results.

☆ 3 PRIORITY GOALS

1. ....
2. ....
3. ....

Self-Care Check

○ **PHYSICAL**
Move or rest.

○ **SOCIAL**
Quality conversation.

○ **SPIRITUAL**
Good for the soul.

○ **HOUSEHOLD**
Cleaning or organizing.

○ **PAMPERING**
Treat yourself.

○ **PERSONAL**
Time on a hobby.

○ **EMOTIONAL**
Honor feelings.

○ **MENTAL**
Read or learn.

💭 MY THOUGHTS & NOTES

....
....
....
....
....

Choose your life from a place of joy, not fear, and never settle.

🌿 GRATITUDE CHECK

TONIGHT I AM GRATEFUL FOR . . .

1. ....

2. ....

3. ....

Wellness Check

○ WORKOUT   ○ NATURE
○ MEDITATION   CAFFEINE: ....
○ NUTRITION   STEPS: ....

WATER INTAKE:

🥛 🥛 🥛 🥛 🥛 🥛 🥛

🧠 MENTAL HEALTH CHECK

RIGHT NOW I FEEL . . . (YOU MAY CHOOSE MORE THAN ONE)

○ HAPPY	○ PEACEFUL	○ PROUD
○ LOVING	○ CREATIVE	○ SAD
○ HOPEFUL	○ STRESSED	○ TIRED
○ CALM	○ ANNOYED	○ SCARED
○ ANGRY	○ POSITIVE	○ JOYFUL
○ OVERWHELMED	○ ANXIOUS	○ ....

WHAT DO YOU WISH YOU COULD STOP WORRYING ABOUT? HOW CAN YOU SOLVE IT?

....

....

....

🏆 WINS FOR THE DAY

TODAY I ACCOMPLISHED . . .

....

....

....

....

💭 MY THOUGHTS & NOTES

....

....

....

....

....

What is meant for you is ready for you. It will make its way to you.
Never stop believing.

I FEEL . . . 😄 😍 😴 🙁 😟 😣   I WANT TO FEEL ....

🧠 GRATITUDE CHECK

TODAY I AM GRATEFUL FOR . . .

1. ....

2. ....

3. ....

**IT IS TOO MUCH OF A
BURDEN TO DWELL IN
THE PAST FOR TOO LONG.
REMEMBER THE PAST,
BUT HAVE FAITH IN
THE PRESENT.**

☀️ DAILY AFFIRMATIONS

1. ....

2. ....

3. ....

BONUS: *Read each affirmation 10x in the mirror & throughout the day for faster results.*

☀️ 3 PRIORITY GOALS

1. ....

2. ....

3. ....

Self-Care Check

○ **PHYSICAL**
Move or rest.

○ **SOCIAL**
Quality conversation.

○ **SPIRITUAL**
Good for the soul.

○ **HOUSEHOLD**
Cleaning or organizing.

○ **PAMPERING**
Treat yourself.

○ **PERSONAL**
Time on a hobby.

○ **EMOTIONAL**
Honor feelings.

○ **MENTAL**
Read or learn.

💭 MY THOUGHTS & NOTES

....

....

....

....

EVENING REFLECTIONS

Consistency is the one thing that will get you to where you want to go, yet it's also the one thing that can keep you from where you want to be.

♡ GRATITUDE CHECK

TONIGHT I AM GRATEFUL FOR . . .

1. ....

2. ....

3. ....

Wellness Check

○ WORKOUT   ○ NATURE

○ MEDITATION CAFFEINE: ....

○ NUTRITION   STEPS: ....

WATER INTAKE:

🧠 MENTAL HEALTH CHECK

RIGHT NOW I FEEL . . . (YOU MAY CHOOSE MORE THAN ONE)

○ HAPPY	○ PEACEFUL	○ PROUD
○ LOVING	○ CREATIVE	○ SAD
○ HOPEFUL	○ STRESSED	○ TIRED
○ CALM	○ ANNOYED	○ SCARED
○ ANGRY	○ POSITIVE	○ JOYFUL
○ OVERWHELMED	○ ANXIOUS	○ ....

HOW COULD YOU ADD MORE PLAY INTO YOUR DAY?

....

....

....

🏆 WINS FOR THE DAY

TODAY I ACCOMPLISHED . . .

....

....

....

....

💭 MY THOUGHTS & NOTES

....

....

....

....

....

MORNING INTENTIONS

You don't become what you want; you become who you believe you are.

I FEEL . . . 😃 😍 😑💤 🙁 😟 😣   I WANT TO FEEL ....

🫶 GRATITUDE CHECK

TODAY I AM GRATEFUL FOR . . .

1. ....

2. ....

3. ....

IT'S SO EASY TO LOOK IN THE MIRROR AND CRITICIZE YOURSELF FOR WHAT YOU DON'T LIKE. INSTEAD OF HATING, GIVE YOURSELF LOVE AND AT LEAST ONE COMPLIMENT A DAY.

💡 DAILY AFFIRMATIONS

1. ....

2. ....

3. ....

BONUS: *Read each affirmation 10x in the mirror & throughout the day for faster results.*

☀️ 3 PRIORITY GOALS

1. ....

2. ....

3. ....

☁️ MY THOUGHTS & NOTES

Self-Care Check

- ⚪ **PHYSICAL**
  Move or rest.
- ⚪ **SOCIAL**
  Quality conversation.
- ⚪ **SPIRITUAL**
  Good for the soul.
- ⚪ **HOUSEHOLD**
  Cleaning or organizing.
- ⚪ **PAMPERING**
  Treat yourself.
- ⚪ **PERSONAL**
  Time on a hobby.
- ⚪ **EMOTIONAL**
  Honor feelings.
- ⚪ **MENTAL**
  Read or learn.

....

....

....

....

Great things happen when you don't give up. Keep going, stay positive, and stay grateful.

GRATITUDE CHECK

TONIGHT I AM GRATEFUL FOR . . .

1. ....

2. ....

3. ....

Wellness Check

- ○ **WORKOUT**   ○ **NATURE**
- ○ **MEDITATION**   **CAFFEINE:** ....
- ○ **NUTRITION**   **STEPS:** ....

WATER INTAKE:

MENTAL HEALTH CHECK

RIGHT NOW I FEEL . . . (YOU MAY CHOOSE MORE THAN ONE)

○ HAPPY	○ PEACEFUL	○ PROUD
○ LOVING	○ CREATIVE	○ SAD
○ HOPEFUL	○ STRESSED	○ TIRED
○ CALM	○ ANNOYED	○ SCARED
○ ANGRY	○ POSITIVE	○ JOYFUL
○ OVERWHELMED	○ ANXIOUS	○ ....

WHAT IS SOMETHING YOU HAVE ALWAYS WANTED TO TRY, BUT NEVER HAVE?

....

....

....

WINS FOR THE DAY

TODAY I ACCOMPLISHED . . .

....

....

....

MY THOUGHTS & NOTES

....

....

....

....

....

Happiness is not the absence of problems. It's the ability to deal with them. —Steve Maraboli

I FEEL . . . 😄 😍 😴 🙁 😢 😣   I WANT TO FEEL ....

❤️ GRATITUDE CHECK

TODAY I AM GRATEFUL FOR . . .

1. ....

2. ....

3. ....

**THINK OF 3 THINGS
YOU CAN DO TO BRING
HAPPINESS INTO YOUR
DAY . . . GO!**

💡 DAILY AFFIRMATIONS

1. ....

2. ....

3. ....

BONUS: *Read each affirmation 10x in the mirror & throughout the day for faster results.*

☆ 3 PRIORITY GOALS

1. ....

2. ....

3. ....

💭 MY THOUGHTS & NOTES

Self-Care Check

○ **PHYSICAL**
Move or rest.

○ **SOCIAL**
Quality conversation.

○ **SPIRITUAL**
Good for the soul.

○ **HOUSEHOLD**
Cleaning or organizing.

○ **PAMPERING**
Treat yourself.

○ **PERSONAL**
Time on a hobby.

○ **EMOTIONAL**
Honor feelings.

○ **MENTAL**
Read or learn.

....
....
....
....
....

When things are falling apart, they may actually be falling into place.

🫖 GRATITUDE CHECK

TONIGHT I AM GRATEFUL FOR . . .

1. ....

2. ....

3. ....

🧠 MENTAL HEALTH CHECK

RIGHT NOW I FEEL . . . (YOU MAY CHOOSE MORE THAN ONE)

○ HAPPY	○ PEACEFUL	○ PROUD
○ LOVING	○ CREATIVE	○ SAD
○ HOPEFUL	○ STRESSED	○ TIRED
○ CALM	○ ANNOYED	○ SCARED
○ ANGRY	○ POSITIVE	○ JOYFUL
○ OVERWHELMED	○ ANXIOUS	○ ....

Wellness Check

○ WORKOUT ○ NATURE
○ MEDITATION CAFFEINE: ....
○ NUTRITION STEPS: ....

WATER INTAKE:

🥛 🥛 🥛 🥛 🥛 🥛 🥛

WHAT DO YOU VALUE MOST?
WHO DO YOU VALUE MOST?

....

....

....

🏆 WINS FOR THE DAY

TODAY I ACCOMPLISHED . . .

....

....

....

....

💭 MY THOUGHTS & NOTES

....

....

....

....

....

Sometimes, we're tested not to show our weaknesses, but to discover our strengths.

I FEEL . . . 😄 😍 😴 🙁 😢 😣   I WANT TO FEEL ....

🫶 GRATITUDE CHECK

TODAY I AM GRATEFUL FOR . . .

1. ....
2. ....
3. ....

CONCENTRATE YOUR EFFORTS ON WHAT YOU CAN DO TO IMPROVE A SITUATION. BLAME DOESN'T SERVE ANYONE AND IS A WASTE OF ENERGY.

💡 DAILY AFFIRMATIONS

1. ....
2. ....
3. ....

BONUS: *Read each affirmation 10x in the mirror & throughout the day for faster results.*

☀ 3 PRIORITY GOALS

1. ....
2. ....
3. ....

Self-Care Check

- ○ **PHYSICAL**
  Move or rest.
- ○ **SOCIAL**
  Quality conversation.
- ○ **SPIRITUAL**
  Good for the soul.
- ○ **HOUSEHOLD**
  Cleaning or organizing.
- ○ **PAMPERING**
  Treat yourself.
- ○ **PERSONAL**
  Time on a hobby.
- ○ **EMOTIONAL**
  Honor feelings.
- ○ **MENTAL**
  Read or learn.

💭 MY THOUGHTS & NOTES

....
....
....
....
....

Note to self: I am doing the best I can. It's okay to smile knowing that and be happy.

♡ GRATITUDE CHECK

TONIGHT I AM GRATEFUL FOR . . .

1. ....

2. ....

3. ....

Wellness Check

○ WORKOUT   ○ NATURE

○ MEDITATION   CAFFEINE: ....

○ NUTRITION   STEPS: ....

WATER INTAKE:

🧠 MENTAL HEALTH CHECK

RIGHT NOW I FEEL . . . (YOU MAY CHOOSE MORE THAN ONE)

○ HAPPY	○ PEACEFUL	○ PROUD
○ LOVING	○ CREATIVE	○ SAD
○ HOPEFUL	○ STRESSED	○ TIRED
○ CALM	○ ANNOYED	○ SCARED
○ ANGRY	○ POSITIVE	○ JOYFUL
○ OVERWHELMED	○ ANXIOUS	○ ....

WHAT'S YOUR BIGGEST PRIORITY THIS MONTH?

....

....

....

🏆 WINS FOR THE DAY

TODAY I ACCOMPLISHED . . .

....

....

....

....

💭 MY THOUGHTS & NOTES

....

....

....

....

....

....

MORNING INTENTIONS

Write it in your heart that every day is the best day of the year.
—Ralph Waldo Emerson

I FEEL . . . 😃 😍 😴 🙁 😣 😖   I WANT TO FEEL ....

❤️ GRATITUDE CHECK

TODAY I AM GRATEFUL FOR . . .

1. ....

2. ....

3. ....

**SPEND A FEW MINUTES
TODAY WITH YOUR BARE
FEET ON THE GROUND.
IT'S AN AMAZING WAY
TO RELEASE NEGATIVE
ENERGY.**

💡 DAILY AFFIRMATIONS

1. ....

2. ....

3. ....

BONUS: *Read each affirmation 10x in the mirror & throughout the day for faster results.*

☀️ 3 PRIORITY GOALS

1. ....

2. ....

3. ....

Self-Care Check

○ **PHYSICAL**   ○ **SOCIAL**
Move or rest.   Quality conversation.

○ **SPIRITUAL**   ○ **HOUSEHOLD**
Good for the soul.   Cleaning or organizing.

○ **PAMPERING**   ○ **PERSONAL**
Treat yourself.   Time on a hobby.

○ **EMOTIONAL**   ○ **MENTAL**
Honor feelings.   Read or learn.

☁️ MY THOUGHTS & NOTES

....

....

....

....

....

Once you replace negative thoughts with positive ones, you'll start having positive results. —Willie Nelson

💗 GRATITUDE CHECK

TONIGHT I AM GRATEFUL FOR . . .

1. ....
2. ....
3. ....

Wellness Check

○ WORKOUT   ○ NATURE
○ MEDITATION   CAFFEINE: ....
○ NUTRITION   STEPS: ....

WATER INTAKE:

🥛 🥛 🥛 🥛 🥛 🥛 🥛

🧠 MENTAL HEALTH CHECK

RIGHT NOW I FEEL . . . (YOU MAY CHOOSE MORE THAN ONE)

○ HAPPY	○ PEACEFUL	○ PROUD
○ LOVING	○ CREATIVE	○ SAD
○ HOPEFUL	○ STRESSED	○ TIRED
○ CALM	○ ANNOYED	○ SCARED
○ ANGRY	○ POSITIVE	○ JOYFUL
○ OVERWHELMED	○ ANXIOUS	○ ....

WHAT MAKES YOU FEEL THE MOST AT PEACE? PRIORITIZE THIS TODAY!

....
....
....

🏆 WINS FOR THE DAY

TODAY I ACCOMPLISHED . . .

....
....
....

💭 MY THOUGHTS & NOTES

....
....
....
....
....

One step at a time, one day at a time, and one habit at a time.

I FEEL . . . 😄 😍 😐 🙁 ☹️ 😣   I WANT TO FEEL ....

🫶 GRATITUDE CHECK

TODAY I AM GRATEFUL FOR . . .

1. ....
2. ....
3. ....

STUDIES SHOW THAT MEDITATION REDUCES ANXIETY. CONSIDER STARTING AND/OR ENDING YOUR DAY WITH MEDITATION.

🧠 DAILY AFFIRMATIONS

1. ....
2. ....
3. ....

BONUS: *Read each affirmation 10x in the mirror & throughout the day for faster results.*

☆ 3 PRIORITY GOALS

1. ....
2. ....
3. ....

Self-Care Check

- ○ **PHYSICAL**
  Move or rest.
- ○ **SOCIAL**
  Quality conversation.
- ○ **SPIRITUAL**
  Good for the soul.
- ○ **HOUSEHOLD**
  Cleaning or organizing.
- ○ **PAMPERING**
  Treat yourself.
- ○ **PERSONAL**
  Time on a hobby.
- ○ **EMOTIONAL**
  Honor feelings.
- ○ **MENTAL**
  Read or learn.

💭 MY THOUGHTS & NOTES

....
....
....
....
....

Positive thinking will let you do everything better than negative thinking will. —Zig Ziglar

🏵 GRATITUDE CHECK

TONIGHT I AM GRATEFUL FOR . . .

1. ....
2. ....
3. ....

🧠 MENTAL HEALTH CHECK

RIGHT NOW I FEEL . . . (YOU MAY CHOOSE MORE THAN ONE)

○ HAPPY	○ PEACEFUL	○ PROUD
○ LOVING	○ CREATIVE	○ SAD
○ HOPEFUL	○ STRESSED	○ TIRED
○ CALM	○ ANNOYED	○ SCARED
○ ANGRY	○ POSITIVE	○ JOYFUL
○ OVERWHELMED	○ ANXIOUS	○ _____

Wellness Check

○ WORKOUT   ○ NATURE
○ MEDITATION CAFFEINE: _____
○ NUTRITION   STEPS: _____

WATER INTAKE:

🥛 🥛 🥛 🥛 🥛 🥛 🥛

WHY DO YOU LIVE WHERE YOU DO?

....
....
....

🏆 WINS FOR THE DAY

TODAY I ACCOMPLISHED . . .

....
....
....
....

💭 MY THOUGHTS & NOTES

....
....
....
....
....

All your dreams can come true if you have the courage to pursue them. —Walt Disney

I FEEL . . . 😄 😍 😐 🙁 ☹️ 😣   I WANT TO FEEL ....

💗 GRATITUDE CHECK

TODAY I AM GRATEFUL FOR . . .

1. ....

2. ....

3. ....

💡 DAILY AFFIRMATIONS

1. ....

2. ....

3. ....

BONUS: *Read each affirmation 10x in the mirror & throughout the day for faster results.*

SEEK OUT THE MEDIA THAT WILL UPLIFT AND REJUVENATE YOUR MIND. YOU SHOULD FEEL MOTIVATED AND ENCOURAGED, NOT DEPLETED AND FULL OF DESPAIR.

☆ 3 PRIORITY GOALS

1. ....

2. ....

3. ....

💭 MY THOUGHTS & NOTES

....

....

....

....

....

Self-Care Check

○ **PHYSICAL**
Move or rest.

○ **SOCIAL**
Quality conversation.

○ **SPIRITUAL**
Good for the soul.

○ **HOUSEHOLD**
Cleaning or organizing.

○ **PAMPERING**
Treat yourself.

○ **PERSONAL**
Time on a hobby.

○ **EMOTIONAL**
Honor feelings.

○ **MENTAL**
Read or learn.

The secret ingredient to happiness is repetition of positive thought patterns.

GRATITUDE CHECK

TONIGHT I AM GRATEFUL FOR . . .

1. ....
2. ....
3. ....

MENTAL HEALTH CHECK

RIGHT NOW I FEEL . . . (YOU MAY CHOOSE MORE THAN ONE)

○ HAPPY	○ PEACEFUL	○ PROUD
○ LOVING	○ CREATIVE	○ SAD
○ HOPEFUL	○ STRESSED	○ TIRED
○ CALM	○ ANNOYED	○ SCARED
○ ANGRY	○ POSITIVE	○ JOYFUL
○ OVERWHELMED	○ ANXIOUS	○ ....

Wellness Check

○ WORKOUT   ○ NATURE
○ MEDITATION   CAFFEINE: ....
○ NUTRITION   STEPS: ....

WATER INTAKE:

WHAT'S A SIMPLE HABIT YOU PRACTICE DAILY THAT HELPS YOU STAY POSITIVE?

....
....
....

WINS FOR THE DAY

TODAY I ACCOMPLISHED . . .

....
....
....
....

MY THOUGHTS & NOTES

....
....
....
....
....

DATE: _____ / _____ / _____

In every day, there are 1,440 minutes. That means we have 1,440 daily opportunities to make a positive impact. —Les Brown

I FEEL . . . 😄😍😴☹️😣😖   I WANT TO FEEL ....

🌹 GRATITUDE CHECK

TODAY I AM GRATEFUL FOR . . .

1. ....

2. ....

3. ....

CREATIVITY OPENS THE MIND. SEEK OUT THE THINGS THAT YOU ENJOY DOING AND SPEND MORE TIME DOING THEM.

💡 DAILY AFFIRMATIONS

1. ....

2. ....

3. ....

BONUS: *Read each affirmation 10x in the mirror & throughout the day for faster results.*

☀️ 3 PRIORITY GOALS

1. ....

2. ....

3. ....

Self-Care Check

○ **PHYSICAL**
Move or rest.

○ **SOCIAL**
Quality conversation.

○ **SPIRITUAL**
Good for the soul.

○ **HOUSEHOLD**
Cleaning or organizing.

○ **PAMPERING**
Treat yourself.

○ **PERSONAL**
Time on a hobby.

○ **EMOTIONAL**
Honor feelings.

○ **MENTAL**
Read or learn.

💭 MY THOUGHTS & NOTES

....

....

....

....

The way I see it, if you want the rainbow, you gotta put up with the rain. —Dolly Parton

GRATITUDE CHECK

TONIGHT I AM GRATEFUL FOR . . .

1. ....
2. ....
3. ....

Wellness Check

○ **WORKOUT**   ○ **NATURE**

○ **MEDITATION** **CAFFEINE:** ....

○ **NUTRITION**   **STEPS:** ....

WATER INTAKE:

MENTAL HEALTH CHECK

RIGHT NOW I FEEL . . . (YOU MAY CHOOSE MORE THAN ONE)

○ HAPPY	○ PEACEFUL	○ PROUD
○ LOVING	○ CREATIVE	○ SAD
○ HOPEFUL	○ STRESSED	○ TIRED
○ CALM	○ ANNOYED	○ SCARED
○ ANGRY	○ POSITIVE	○ JOYFUL
○ OVERWHELMED	○ ANXIOUS	○ ....

WHAT WORDS DO YOU WANT TO ELIMINATE FROM YOUR VOCABULARY?

....
....
....

WINS FOR THE DAY

TODAY I ACCOMPLISHED . . .

....
....
....
....

MY THOUGHTS & NOTES

....
....
....
....
....

The more you praise and celebrate your life, the more there is in life to celebrate. —Oprah Winfrey

I FEEL . . . 😄 😍 😴 😕 😣 😖   I WANT TO FEEL ....

❤️ GRATITUDE CHECK

TODAY I AM GRATEFUL FOR . . .

1. ....

2. ....

3. ....

SOCIETY MAY TELL YOU THEIR DEFINITION OF SUCCESS, BUT YOU DON'T NEED TO LISTEN. FIND OUT WHAT IT MEANS TO YOU, AND MOVE TOWARD THAT.

💡 DAILY AFFIRMATIONS

1. ....

2. ....

3. ....

BONUS: *Read each affirmation 10x in the mirror & throughout the day for faster results.*

☆ 3 PRIORITY GOALS

1. ....

2. ....

3. ....

Self-Care Check

○ **PHYSICAL**
Move or rest.

○ **SOCIAL**
Quality conversation.

○ **SPIRITUAL**
Good for the soul.

○ **HOUSEHOLD**
Cleaning or organizing.

○ **PAMPERING**
Treat yourself.

○ **PERSONAL**
Time on a hobby.

○ **EMOTIONAL**
Honor feelings.

○ **MENTAL**
Read or learn.

💭 MY THOUGHTS & NOTES

....

....

....

....

....

EVENING REFLECTIONS

Happy people have created a habit of the good sense of not dwelling on their mistakes.

❤️ GRATITUDE CHECK

TONIGHT I AM GRATEFUL FOR . . .

1. ....

2. ....

3. ....

🧠 MENTAL HEALTH CHECK

RIGHT NOW I FEEL . . . (YOU MAY CHOOSE MORE THAN ONE)

○ HAPPY	○ PEACEFUL	○ PROUD
○ LOVING	○ CREATIVE	○ SAD
○ HOPEFUL	○ STRESSED	○ TIRED
○ CALM	○ ANNOYED	○ SCARED
○ ANGRY	○ POSITIVE	○ JOYFUL
○ OVERWHELMED	○ ANXIOUS	○ ....

Wellness Check

○ WORKOUT   ○ NATURE
○ MEDITATION   CAFFEINE: ....
○ NUTRITION   STEPS: ....

WATER INTAKE:

THINK ABOUT THE LAST TIME YOU CRIED HAPPY TEARS, WHY?

....

....

....

🏆 WINS FOR THE DAY

TODAY I ACCOMPLISHED . . .

....

....

....

....

💭 MY THOUGHTS & NOTES

....

....

....

....

....

The good life is a process, not a state of being. It is a direction, not a destination. —Carl Rogers

I FEEL . . . 😋 😍 😑 😟 😢 😣   I WANT TO FEEL ....

💚 GRATITUDE CHECK

TODAY I AM GRATEFUL FOR . . .

1. ....

2. ....

3. ....

SET POSITIVE HABITS BEFORE BED. READ A BOOK, LISTEN TO SOFT MUSIC, RECITE YOUR AFFIRMATIONS. GOING TO BED HAPPY CAN HELP YOU WAKE UP HAPPY.

🧠 DAILY AFFIRMATIONS

1. ....

2. ....

3. ....

BONUS: *Read each affirmation 10x in the mirror & throughout the day for faster results.*

☀ 3 PRIORITY GOALS

1. ....

2. ....

3. ....

💭 MY THOUGHTS & NOTES

Self-Care Check

○ **PHYSICAL**
Move or rest.

○ **SOCIAL**
Quality conversation.

○ **SPIRITUAL**
Good for the soul.

○ **HOUSEHOLD**
Cleaning or organizing.

○ **PAMPERING**
Treat yourself.

○ **PERSONAL**
Time on a hobby.

○ **EMOTIONAL**
Honor feelings.

○ **MENTAL**
Read or learn.

....

....

....

....

Staying positive does not mean everything will turn out okay. Rather, it means you will be okay no matter how things turn out.

♡ GRATITUDE CHECK

TONIGHT I AM GRATEFUL FOR . . .

1. ....

2. ....

3. ....

Wellness Check

○ WORKOUT   ○ NATURE

○ MEDITATION CAFFEINE: ....

○ NUTRITION STEPS: ....

WATER INTAKE:

🧠 MENTAL HEALTH CHECK

RIGHT NOW I FEEL . . . (YOU MAY CHOOSE MORE THAN ONE)

○ HAPPY   ○ PEACEFUL   ○ PROUD
○ LOVING   ○ CREATIVE   ○ SAD
○ HOPEFUL   ○ STRESSED   ○ TIRED
○ CALM   ○ ANNOYED   ○ SCARED
○ ANGRY   ○ POSITIVE   ○ JOYFUL
○ OVERWHELMED   ○ ANXIOUS   ○ ....

YOUR PAST DOESN'T DEFINE WHO YOU ARE BECAUSE . . .

....

....

....

🏆 WINS FOR THE DAY

TODAY I ACCOMPLISHED . . .

....

....

....

....

💭 MY THOUGHTS & NOTES

....

....

....

....

....

If you have a choice in friends, choose happy ones. Those who also celebrate your happiness.

I FEEL . . . 😄 😍 😐 🙁 😣 😖   I WANT TO FEEL ....

❤️ GRATITUDE CHECK

TODAY I AM GRATEFUL FOR . . .

1. ....

2. ....

3. ....

SCHEDULE SOME TIME THIS WEEK TO NOT THINK ABOUT WORK. GIVE YOUR MIND A BREAK.

💡 DAILY AFFIRMATIONS

1. ....

2. ....

3. ....

BONUS: *Read each affirmation 10x in the mirror & throughout the day for faster results.*

☆ 3 PRIORITY GOALS

1. ....

2. ....

3. ....

☁️ MY THOUGHTS & NOTES

Self-Care Check

○ **PHYSICAL**
Move or rest.

○ **SOCIAL**
Quality conversation.

○ **SPIRITUAL**
Good for the soul.

○ **HOUSEHOLD**
Cleaning or organizing.

○ **PAMPERING**
Treat yourself.

○ **PERSONAL**
Time on a hobby.

○ **EMOTIONAL**
Honor feelings.

○ **MENTAL**
Read or learn.

....
....
....
....
....

Nobody can go back and start a new beginning, but anyone can start today and make a new ending. —Maria Robinson

GRATITUDE CHECK

TONIGHT I AM GRATEFUL FOR . . .

1. ....

2. ....

3. ....

Wellness Check

○ WORKOUT   ○ NATURE

○ MEDITATION CAFFEINE: ....

○ NUTRITION   STEPS: ....

WATER INTAKE:

MENTAL HEALTH CHECK

RIGHT NOW I FEEL . . . (YOU MAY CHOOSE MORE THAN ONE)

○ HAPPY	○ PEACEFUL	○ PROUD
○ LOVING	○ CREATIVE	○ SAD
○ HOPEFUL	○ STRESSED	○ TIRED
○ CALM	○ ANNOYED	○ SCARED
○ ANGRY	○ POSITIVE	○ JOYFUL
○ OVERWHELMED	○ ANXIOUS	○ ....

WHAT DOES YOUR INNER CHILD MOST NEED YOU TO SAY TO HIM/HER?

....

....

....

WINS FOR THE DAY

TODAY I ACCOMPLISHED . . .

....

....

....

....

MY THOUGHTS & NOTES

....

....

....

....

....

Just believe in yourself. Even if you don't, pretend that you do and, at some point, you will. —Venus Williams

---

I FEEL . . . 😄 😍 😴 🙁 😢 😣   I WANT TO FEEL ....

💚 GRATITUDE CHECK

TODAY I AM GRATEFUL FOR . . .

1. ....

2. ....

3. ....

NEED A QUICK PICK-ME-UP? CLOSE YOUR EYES AND VISUALIZE THE THINGS AND PEOPLE THAT MAKE YOU HAPPY.

💡 DAILY AFFIRMATIONS

1. ....

2. ....

3. ....

BONUS: *Read each affirmation 10x in the mirror & throughout the day for faster results.*

☆ 3 PRIORITY GOALS

1. ....

2. ....

3. ....

Self-Care Check

○ **PHYSICAL**
Move or rest.

○ **SOCIAL**
Quality conversation.

○ **SPIRITUAL**
Good for the soul.

○ **HOUSEHOLD**
Cleaning or organizing.

○ **PAMPERING**
Treat yourself.

○ **PERSONAL**
Time on a hobby.

○ **EMOTIONAL**
Honor feelings.

○ **MENTAL**
Read or learn.

💭 MY THOUGHTS & NOTES

....

....

....

....

....

Find peace in your heart and you'll find it in the world.

🌹 GRATITUDE CHECK

TONIGHT I AM GRATEFUL FOR . . .

1. ....

2. ....

3. ....

Wellness Check

○ WORKOUT   ○ NATURE
○ MEDITATION CAFFEINE: ....
○ NUTRITION   STEPS: ....

WATER INTAKE:

🧠 MENTAL HEALTH CHECK

RIGHT NOW I FEEL . . . (YOU MAY CHOOSE MORE THAN ONE)

○ HAPPY   ○ PEACEFUL   ○ PROUD
○ LOVING   ○ CREATIVE   ○ SAD
○ HOPEFUL   ○ STRESSED   ○ TIRED
○ CALM   ○ ANNOYED   ○ SCARED
○ ANGRY   ○ POSITIVE   ○ JOYFUL
○ OVERWHELMED   ○ ANXIOUS   ○ ....

HOW CAN YOU BE KINDER TO YOURSELF?

....

....

....

🏆 WINS FOR THE DAY

TODAY I ACCOMPLISHED . . .

....

....

....

....

💭 MY THOUGHTS & NOTES

....

....

....

....

....

Work hard and believe in yourself even when nobody else believes in you. —Richard Sherman

I FEEL . . . 😄 😍 😴 🙁 😣 😖   I WANT TO FEEL ....

❤ GRATITUDE CHECK

TODAY I AM GRATEFUL FOR . . .

1. ....

2. ....

3. ....

IF IT FEELS HARD TO BE POSITIVE TODAY, LET YOURSELF PROCESS THE QUESTION "WHY?" SIFT THROUGH YOUR EMOTIONS FIRST AND KNOW THAT IT'S TEMPORARY.

🖤 DAILY AFFIRMATIONS

1. ....

2. ....

3. ....

BONUS: *Read each affirmation 10x in the mirror & throughout the day for faster results.*

☆ 3 PRIORITY GOALS

1. ....

2. ....

3. ....

Self-Care Check

○ **PHYSICAL**
Move or rest.

○ **SOCIAL**
Quality conversation.

○ **SPIRITUAL**
Good for the soul.

○ **HOUSEHOLD**
Cleaning or organizing.

○ **PAMPERING**
Treat yourself.

○ **PERSONAL**
Time on a hobby.

○ **EMOTIONAL**
Honor feelings.

○ **MENTAL**
Read or learn.

☁ MY THOUGHTS & NOTES

....

....

....

....

Problems exist, because without them there would be no need for solutions. Trust in a solution to the problem you are facing right now.

❤ GRATITUDE CHECK

TONIGHT I AM GRATEFUL FOR . . .

1. ....

2. ....

3. ....

Wellness Check

- ○ **WORKOUT**   ○ **NATURE**
- ○ **MEDITATION** **CAFFEINE:** ....
- ○ **NUTRITION**   **STEPS:** ....

WATER INTAKE:

🥛 🥛 🥛 🥛 🥛 🥛 🥛

🧠 MENTAL HEALTH CHECK

RIGHT NOW I FEEL . . . (YOU MAY CHOOSE MORE THAN ONE)

○ HAPPY	○ PEACEFUL	○ PROUD
○ LOVING	○ CREATIVE	○ SAD
○ HOPEFUL	○ STRESSED	○ TIRED
○ CALM	○ ANNOYED	○ SCARED
○ ANGRY	○ POSITIVE	○ JOYFUL
○ OVERWHELMED	○ ANXIOUS	○ ....

WHEN WERE YOU FULLY IN THE MOMENT TODAY?

....

....

....

🏆 WINS FOR THE DAY

TODAY I ACCOMPLISHED . . .

....

....

....

....

💭 MY THOUGHTS & NOTES

....

....

....

....

....

What happens next is up to you. —Chris Sacca

I FEEL . . . 😄 😍 😑💤 🙁 😟 😣   I WANT TO FEEL ....

💗 GRATITUDE CHECK

TODAY I AM GRATEFUL FOR . . .

1. ....

2. ....

3. ....

STUDIES SHOW THAT EXERCISING IN NATURE REDUCES ANXIETY. CONSIDER STARTING AND/ OR ENDING YOUR DAY WITH A WALK OUTSIDE.

💡 DAILY AFFIRMATIONS

1. ....

2. ....

3. ....

BONUS: *Read each affirmation 10x in the mirror & throughout the day for faster results.*

☼ 3 PRIORITY GOALS

1. ....

2. ....

3. ....

Self-Care Check

- ○ **PHYSICAL**
  Move or rest.
- ○ **SOCIAL**
  Quality conversation.
- ○ **SPIRITUAL**
  Good for the soul.
- ○ **HOUSEHOLD**
  Cleaning or organizing.
- ○ **PAMPERING**
  Treat yourself.
- ○ **PERSONAL**
  Time on a hobby.
- ○ **EMOTIONAL**
  Honor feelings.
- ○ **MENTAL**
  Read or learn.

💭 MY THOUGHTS & NOTES

....

....

....

....

....

EVENING REFLECTIONS

The secret ingredient to life well lived is a positive, grateful mindset.

🌹 GRATITUDE CHECK

TONIGHT I AM GRATEFUL FOR . . .

1. ....
2. ....
3. ....

Wellness Check

○ WORKOUT ○ NATURE
○ MEDITATION CAFFEINE: ....
○ NUTRITION STEPS: ....

WATER INTAKE:

🧠 MENTAL HEALTH CHECK

RIGHT NOW I FEEL . . . (YOU MAY CHOOSE MORE THAN ONE)

○ HAPPY	○ PEACEFUL	○ PROUD
○ LOVING	○ CREATIVE	○ SAD
○ HOPEFUL	○ STRESSED	○ TIRED
○ CALM	○ ANNOYED	○ SCARED
○ ANGRY	○ POSITIVE	○ JOYFUL
○ OVERWHELMED	○ ANXIOUS	○ ....

IF YOU LET YOUR THOUGHTS WANDER, WHAT MEMORY COMES TO MIND FIRST?

....

....

....

🏆 WINS FOR THE DAY

TODAY I ACCOMPLISHED . . .

....

....

....

....

💭 MY THOUGHTS & NOTES

....

....

....

....

....

....

MORNING INTENTIONS

I don't know what the future may hold, but I know who holds the future. —Ralph Abernathy

I FEEL . . . 😄 😍 😐 😦 😣 😫   I WANT TO FEEL ....

🌿 GRATITUDE CHECK

TODAY I AM GRATEFUL FOR . . .

1. ....
2. ....
3. ....

IF YOU CAN'T GET OUT IN NATURE, CONSIDER BRINGING NATURE TO YOU. A FRESH BOUQUET OF FLOWERS CAN BRIGHTEN YOUR HOME OR OFFICE AND MOOD.

💡 DAILY AFFIRMATIONS

1. ....
2. ....
3. ....

BONUS: *Read each affirmation 10x in the mirror & throughout the day for faster results.*

☼ 3 PRIORITY GOALS

1. ....
2. ....
3. ....

💭 MY THOUGHTS & NOTES

Self-Care Check

- ○ **PHYSICAL**
  Move or rest.
- ○ **SPIRITUAL**
  Good for the soul.
- ○ **PAMPERING**
  Treat yourself.
- ○ **EMOTIONAL**
  Honor feelings.
- ○ **SOCIAL**
  Quality conversation.
- ○ **HOUSEHOLD**
  Cleaning or organizing.
- ○ **PERSONAL**
  Time on a hobby.
- ○ **MENTAL**
  Read or learn.

....
....
....
....

EVENING REFLECTIONS

Living a happy life is not about ignoring negative emotions. It's about being aware of them and transforming them.

🫀 GRATITUDE CHECK

TONIGHT I AM GRATEFUL FOR . . .

1. ....

2. ....

3. ....

Wellness Check

○ **WORKOUT**   ○ **NATURE**

○ **MEDITATION**   CAFFEINE: ....

○ **NUTRITION**   STEPS: ....

WATER INTAKE:

🥛 🥛 🥛 🥛 🥛 🥛 🥛

🧠 MENTAL HEALTH CHECK

RIGHT NOW I FEEL . . . (YOU MAY CHOOSE MORE THAN ONE)

○ HAPPY	○ PEACEFUL	○ PROUD
○ LOVING	○ CREATIVE	○ SAD
○ HOPEFUL	○ STRESSED	○ TIRED
○ CALM	○ ANNOYED	○ SCARED
○ ANGRY	○ POSITIVE	○ JOYFUL
○ OVERWHELMED	○ ANXIOUS	○ ....

WHERE DID YOU NOTICE BEAUTY TODAY?

....

....

....

🏆 WINS FOR THE DAY

TODAY I ACCOMPLISHED . . .

....

....

....

....

💭 MY THOUGHTS & NOTES

....

....

....

....

....

Accept what is, let go of what was, and make changes toward what will be. Life's about taking action.

@POSITIVEKRISTEN

HAVE I FELT A BOOST OF HAPPINESS LATELY? ✓ ✗

WHAT HAVE I LEARNED IN THE PAST 30 DAYS?

....

....

....

....

WHAT NEW HABITS HAVE I ACQUIRED?

....

....

....

WHAT CHALLENGES HAVE I HAD TO WORK ON?

....

....

....

WHAT ARE MY NEXT STEPS?

....

....

....

Your emotions are valid. It's what you do with them that can set you back or propel you forward.

I FEEL . . . 😀 😍 😌💤 🙁 🥺 😖   I WANT TO FEEL ....

🌱 GRATITUDE CHECK

TODAY I AM GRATEFUL FOR . . .

1. ....

2. ....

3. ....

💡 DAILY AFFIRMATIONS

1. ....

2. ....

3. ....

BONUS: *Read each affirmation 10x in the mirror & throughout the day for faster results.*

AIM TO EAT FOODS HIGH IN VITAMIN C, B$_6$, AND OMEGA-3s. FOOD NOT ONLY IMPACTS YOUR PHYSICAL HEALTH, BUT HAS A SIGNIFICANT IMPACT ON YOUR MENTAL HEALTH TOO.

☀️ 3 PRIORITY GOALS

1. ....

2. ....

3. ....

☁️ MY THOUGHTS & NOTES

Self-Care Check

- ○ **PHYSICAL**
  Move or rest.
- ○ **SOCIAL**
  Quality conversation.
- ○ **SPIRITUAL**
  Good for the soul.
- ○ **HOUSEHOLD**
  Cleaning or organizing.
- ○ **PAMPERING**
  Treat yourself.
- ○ **PERSONAL**
  Time on a hobby.
- ○ **EMOTIONAL**
  Honor feelings.
- ○ **MENTAL**
  Read or learn.

....

....

....

....

....

DATE: .... / .... / ....

You are the only one who gets to decide what you will be remembered for. —Taylor Swift

---

♡ GRATITUDE CHECK

TONIGHT I AM GRATEFUL FOR . . .

1. ....
2. ....
3. ....

Wellness Check

○ WORKOUT   ○ NATURE
○ MEDITATION CAFFEINE: ....
○ NUTRITION   STEPS: ....

WATER INTAKE:

🧠 MENTAL HEALTH CHECK

RIGHT NOW I FEEL . . . (YOU MAY CHOOSE MORE THAN ONE)

○ HAPPY	○ PEACEFUL	○ PROUD
○ LOVING	○ CREATIVE	○ SAD
○ HOPEFUL	○ STRESSED	○ TIRED
○ CALM	○ ANNOYED	○ SCARED
○ ANGRY	○ POSITIVE	○ JOYFUL
○ OVERWHELMED	○ ANXIOUS	○ ....

WHEN YOU WERE YOUNGER, WHAT DID YOU LIKE TO DO WHEN IT RAINED?

....
....
....
....

🏆 WINS FOR THE DAY

TODAY I ACCOMPLISHED . . .

....
....
....
....

💭 MY THOUGHTS & NOTES

....
....
....
....
....

Desiring to live a happy life is not selfish; it's your birthright. It's pivotal to nurture our mental health and well-being.

I FEEL . . . 😃 😍 😴 ☹️ 😣 😫   I WANT TO FEEL ....

🧠 GRATITUDE CHECK

TODAY I AM GRATEFUL FOR . . .

1. ....

2. ....

3. ....

IF YOU'RE IN A SLUMP, REMEMBER THIS: THERE'S NO SHAME IN NEEDING TO TALK TO A PROFESSIONAL. DON'T HESITATE TO SEEK HELP.

💡 DAILY AFFIRMATIONS

1. ....

2. ....

3. ....

BONUS: *Read each affirmation 10x in the mirror & throughout the day for faster results.*

☀️ 3 PRIORITY GOALS

1. ....

2. ....

3. ....

💭 MY THOUGHTS & NOTES

Self-Care Check

- ○ **PHYSICAL** Move or rest.
- ○ **SOCIAL** Quality conversation.
- ○ **SPIRITUAL** Good for the soul.
- ○ **HOUSEHOLD** Cleaning or organizing.
- ○ **PAMPERING** Treat yourself.
- ○ **PERSONAL** Time on a hobby.
- ○ **EMOTIONAL** Honor feelings.
- ○ **MENTAL** Read or learn.

....

....

....

....

....

EVENING REFLECTIONS

DATE: .... / .... / ....

You don't overcome challenges by making them smaller, but by making yourself bigger. —John C. Maxwell

---

🫶 GRATITUDE CHECK

TONIGHT I AM GRATEFUL FOR . . .

1. ....

2. ....

3. ....

Wellness Check

○ WORKOUT   ○ NATURE
○ MEDITATION   CAFFEINE: ....
○ NUTRITION   STEPS: ....

WATER INTAKE:

🧠 MENTAL HEALTH CHECK

RIGHT NOW I FEEL . . . (YOU MAY CHOOSE MORE THAN ONE)

○ HAPPY	○ PEACEFUL	○ PROUD
○ LOVING	○ CREATIVE	○ SAD
○ HOPEFUL	○ STRESSED	○ TIRED
○ CALM	○ ANNOYED	○ SCARED
○ ANGRY	○ POSITIVE	○ JOYFUL
○ OVERWHELMED	○ ANXIOUS	○ ....

WHAT COULD YOU DO THIS WEEK TO EXPRESS GRATITUDE TO OTHERS?

....

....

....

🏆 WINS FOR THE DAY

TODAY I ACCOMPLISHED . . .

....

....

....

....

💭 MY THOUGHTS & NOTES

....

....

....

....

....

Living a happy life involves learning to find the good even in the waves of change and uncertainty, adjusting our course as needed.

___

I FEEL... 😄😍😴🙁😣😖   I WANT TO FEEL ....

❤ GRATITUDE CHECK

TODAY I AM GRATEFUL FOR...

1. ....

2. ....

3. ....

THINK OF 3 THINGS YOU CAN DO TO BRING LOVE INTO YOUR DAY... GO!

💡 DAILY AFFIRMATIONS

1. ....

2. ....

3. ....

BONUS: *Read each affirmation 10x in the mirror & throughout the day for faster results.*

☀ 3 PRIORITY GOALS

1. ....

2. ....

3. ....

☁ MY THOUGHTS & NOTES

Self-Care Check

○ **PHYSICAL**
Move or rest.

○ **SOCIAL**
Quality conversation.

○ **SPIRITUAL**
Good for the soul.

○ **HOUSEHOLD**
Cleaning or organizing.

○ **PAMPERING**
Treat yourself.

○ **PERSONAL**
Time on a hobby.

○ **EMOTIONAL**
Honor feelings.

○ **MENTAL**
Read or learn.

....

....

....

....

....

I still believe that love is all you need. I don't know a better message than that. —Paul McCartney

🌿 GRATITUDE CHECK

TONIGHT I AM GRATEFUL FOR . . .

1. ....

2. ....

3. ....

Wellness Check

- ○ WORKOUT ○ NATURE
- ○ MEDITATION CAFFEINE: ....
- ○ NUTRITION STEPS: ....

WATER INTAKE:

🧠 MENTAL HEALTH CHECK

RIGHT NOW I FEEL . . . (YOU MAY CHOOSE MORE THAN ONE)

○ HAPPY	○ PEACEFUL	○ PROUD
○ LOVING	○ CREATIVE	○ SAD
○ HOPEFUL	○ STRESSED	○ TIRED
○ CALM	○ ANNOYED	○ SCARED
○ ANGRY	○ POSITIVE	○ JOYFUL
○ OVERWHELMED	○ ANXIOUS	○ ....

HOW HAVE YOU GROWN IN THE PAST YEAR?

....

....

....

....

🏆 WINS FOR THE DAY

TODAY I ACCOMPLISHED . . .

....

....

....

....

💭 MY THOUGHTS & NOTES

....

....

....

....

....

....

If you want to be happy, focus on changing yourself instead of others.

I FEEL . . . 😄 😍 😴 🙁 😖 😣   I WANT TO FEEL ....

🫀 GRATITUDE CHECK

TODAY I AM GRATEFUL FOR . . .

1. ....

2. ....

3. ....

THIS IS YOUR REMINDER TO GIVE YOURSELF A COMPLIMENT NEXT TIME YOU LOOK IN THE MIRROR. IF IT MAKES YOU FEEL GOOD, DO IT EVERY TIME!

💡 DAILY AFFIRMATIONS

1. ....

2. ....

3. ....

BONUS: *Read each affirmation 10x in the mirror & throughout the day for faster results.*

☆ 3 PRIORITY GOALS

1. ....

2. ....

3. ....

Self-Care Check

○ **PHYSICAL**
Move or rest.

○ **SOCIAL**
Quality conversation.

○ **SPIRITUAL**
Good for the soul.

○ **HOUSEHOLD**
Cleaning or organizing.

○ **PAMPERING**
Treat yourself.

○ **PERSONAL**
Time on a hobby.

○ **EMOTIONAL**
Honor feelings.

○ **MENTAL**
Read or learn.

💭 MY THOUGHTS & NOTES

....

....

....

....

....

EVENING REFLECTIONS

What seems to us as bitter trials are often blessings in disguise.
—Oscar Wilde

♡ GRATITUDE CHECK

TONIGHT I AM GRATEFUL FOR . . .

1. ....

2. ....

3. ....

Wellness Check

○ WORKOUT ○ NATURE

○ MEDITATION CAFFEINE: ....

○ NUTRITION STEPS: ....

WATER INTAKE:

🧠 MENTAL HEALTH CHECK

RIGHT NOW I FEEL . . . (YOU MAY CHOOSE MORE THAN ONE)

○ HAPPY	○ PEACEFUL	○ PROUD
○ LOVING	○ CREATIVE	○ SAD
○ HOPEFUL	○ STRESSED	○ TIRED
○ CALM	○ ANNOYED	○ SCARED
○ ANGRY	○ POSITIVE	○ JOYFUL
○ OVERWHELMED	○ ANXIOUS	○ ....

WHAT ARE YOU HOLDING ON TO
TOO TIGHTLY?

....

....

....

🏆 WINS FOR THE DAY

TODAY I ACCOMPLISHED . . .

....

....

....

....

💭 MY THOUGHTS & NOTES

....

....

....

....

....

Some of the most positive people I've met have not been given an easy life. They have created strength and happiness from dark places.

I FEEL . . . 😄 😍 😴 ☹️ 😣 😖   I WANT TO FEEL ....

🫶 GRATITUDE CHECK

TODAY I AM GRATEFUL FOR . . .

1. ....
2. ....
3. ....

BREAK BIG TASKS DOWN INTO SIMPLE STEPS AND JUST DO ONE AT A TIME. OVERWHELM CREATES PROCRASTINATION AND YOU DON'T NEED EITHER RIGHT NOW.

🔅 DAILY AFFIRMATIONS

1. ....
2. ....
3. ....

BONUS: *Read each affirmation 10x in the mirror & throughout the day for faster results.*

☆ 3 PRIORITY GOALS

1. ....
2. ....
3. ....

☁️ MY THOUGHTS & NOTES

Self-Care Check

- ○ **PHYSICAL**
  Move or rest.
- ○ **SOCIAL**
  Quality conversation.
- ○ **SPIRITUAL**
  Good for the soul.
- ○ **HOUSEHOLD**
  Cleaning or organizing.
- ○ **PAMPERING**
  Treat yourself.
- ○ **PERSONAL**
  Time on a hobby.
- ○ **EMOTIONAL**
  Honor feelings.
- ○ **MENTAL**
  Read or learn.

....
....
....
....
....

EVENING REFLECTIONS

We become what we think about most of the time, and that's the strangest secret. —Earl Nightingale

---

🧠 GRATITUDE CHECK

TONIGHT I AM GRATEFUL FOR . . .

1. ....
2. ....
3. ....

Wellness Check

○ WORKOUT   ○ NATURE
○ MEDITATION   CAFFEINE: ....
○ NUTRITION   STEPS: ....

WATER INTAKE:

🧠 MENTAL HEALTH CHECK

RIGHT NOW I FEEL . . . (YOU MAY CHOOSE MORE THAN ONE)

○ HAPPY	○ PEACEFUL	○ PROUD
○ LOVING	○ CREATIVE	○ SAD
○ HOPEFUL	○ STRESSED	○ TIRED
○ CALM	○ ANNOYED	○ SCARED
○ ANGRY	○ POSITIVE	○ JOYFUL
○ OVERWHELMED	○ ANXIOUS	○ ....

WHAT WOULD YOU DO IF YOU
WERE GRANTED THREE WISHES?

....
....
....

🏆 WINS FOR THE DAY

TODAY I ACCOMPLISHED . . .

....
....
....

💭 MY THOUGHTS & NOTES

....
....
....
....
....

Make a decision to talk about why you're blessed, not stressed. You give life to what you focus on.

I FEEL . . . 😄 😍 😌 🙁 😣 😖   I WANT TO FEEL ....

🤍 GRATITUDE CHECK

TODAY I AM GRATEFUL FOR . . .

1. ....
2. ....
3. ....

PUT YOUR PHONE, AND SOCIAL LIFE, INTO SILENT MODE. EVEN GOOD FEELING DISTRACTIONS CAN RUIN YOUR DAY IF YOU LET THEM.

💡 DAILY AFFIRMATIONS

1. ....
2. ....
3. ....

BONUS: *Read each affirmation 10x in the mirror & throughout the day for faster results.*

☀️ 3 PRIORITY GOALS

1. ....
2. ....
3. ....

💭 MY THOUGHTS & NOTES

Self-Care Check

○ **PHYSICAL**
Move or rest.

○ **SOCIAL**
Quality conversation.

○ **SPIRITUAL**
Good for the soul.

○ **HOUSEHOLD**
Cleaning or organizing.

○ **PAMPERING**
Treat yourself.

○ **PERSONAL**
Time on a hobby.

○ **EMOTIONAL**
Honor feelings.

○ **MENTAL**
Read or learn.

....
....
....
....
....

EVENING REFLECTIONS

It's easy to be cynical. It's far more effective to be happy.

♡ GRATITUDE CHECK

TONIGHT I AM GRATEFUL FOR . . .

1. ....

2. ....

3. ....

🧠 MENTAL HEALTH CHECK

RIGHT NOW I FEEL . . . (YOU MAY CHOOSE MORE THAN ONE)

○ HAPPY	○ PEACEFUL	○ PROUD
○ LOVING	○ CREATIVE	○ SAD
○ HOPEFUL	○ STRESSED	○ TIRED
○ CALM	○ ANNOYED	○ SCARED
○ ANGRY	○ POSITIVE	○ JOYFUL
○ OVERWHELMED	○ ANXIOUS	○ ....

Wellness Check

○ WORKOUT   ○ NATURE

○ MEDITATION   CAFFEINE: ....

○ NUTRITION   STEPS: ....

WATER INTAKE:

🥛 🥛 🥛 🥛 🥛 🥛 🥛 🥛

WHAT KIND OF PERSON DO YOU ASPIRE TO BE?

....

....

....

....

🏆 WINS FOR THE DAY

TODAY I ACCOMPLISHED . . .

....

....

....

....

💭 MY THOUGHTS & NOTES

....

....

....

....

....

Two roads diverged in a wood and I, I took the one less traveled by, and that made all the difference. —Robert Frost

I FEEL... 😀 😍 😴 🙁 😣 😖   I WANT TO FEEL ....

🫶 GRATITUDE CHECK

TODAY I AM GRATEFUL FOR . . .

1. ....

2. ....

3. ....

💡 DAILY AFFIRMATIONS

1. ....

2. ....

3. ....

BONUS: *Read each affirmation 10x in the mirror & throughout the day for faster results.*

CONSTANTLY LEARNING SOMETHING NEW THROUGHOUT LIFE MAKES YOU AN INTERESTING AND ALL-AROUND PERSON. IT ALSO KEEPS YOUR BRAIN FROM STAGNATION AS YOU IMPROVE YOUR KNOWLEDGE AND PRACTICE NEW SKILLS.

☀ 3 PRIORITY GOALS

1. ....

2. ....

3. ....

☁ MY THOUGHTS & NOTES

Self-Care Check

○ **PHYSICAL**
Move or rest.

○ **SOCIAL**
Quality conversation.

○ **SPIRITUAL**
Good for the soul.

○ **HOUSEHOLD**
Cleaning or organizing.

○ **PAMPERING**
Treat yourself.

○ **PERSONAL**
Time on a hobby.

○ **EMOTIONAL**
Honor feelings.

○ **MENTAL**
Read or learn.

....

....

....

....

....

DATE: .... / .... / ....

You must expect great things of yourself before you can do them.
—Michael Jordan

♡ GRATITUDE CHECK

TONIGHT I AM GRATEFUL FOR . . .

1. ....

2. ....

3. ....

🧠 MENTAL HEALTH CHECK

RIGHT NOW I FEEL . . . (YOU MAY CHOOSE MORE THAN ONE)

○ HAPPY	○ PEACEFUL	○ PROUD
○ LOVING	○ CREATIVE	○ SAD
○ HOPEFUL	○ STRESSED	○ TIRED
○ CALM	○ ANNOYED	○ SCARED
○ ANGRY	○ POSITIVE	○ JOYFUL
○ OVERWHELMED	○ ANXIOUS	○ ....

Wellness Check

○ WORKOUT   ○ NATURE
○ MEDITATION   CAFFEINE: ....
○ NUTRITION   STEPS: ....

WATER INTAKE:

EVENING GRATITUDE CHECK!
LIST 3 THINGS YOU ARE
THANKFUL FOR . . .

....

....

....

🏆 WINS FOR THE DAY

TODAY I ACCOMPLISHED . . .

....

....

....

....

💭 MY THOUGHTS & NOTES

....

....

....

....

....

People who practice gratitude regularly often seem "lucky" to the outside world. This is a by-product of their grateful attitude.

I FEEL . . . 😄 😍 😴 ☹️ 😖 😣   I WANT TO FEEL ....

🥬 GRATITUDE CHECK

TODAY I AM GRATEFUL FOR . . .

1. ....
2. ....
3. ....

ALWAYS LEARN SOMETHING NEW. YOUR BRAIN WILL GROW AND SO WILL YOU!

💡 DAILY AFFIRMATIONS

1. ....
2. ....
3. ....

BONUS: *Read each affirmation 10x in the mirror & throughout the day for faster results.*

☆ 3 PRIORITY GOALS

1. ....
2. ....
3. ....

☁ MY THOUGHTS & NOTES

Self-Care Check

- ○ **PHYSICAL**
  Move or rest.
- ○ **SOCIAL**
  Quality conversation.
- ○ **SPIRITUAL**
  Good for the soul.
- ○ **HOUSEHOLD**
  Cleaning or organizing.
- ○ **PAMPERING**
  Treat yourself.
- ○ **PERSONAL**
  Time on a hobby.
- ○ **EMOTIONAL**
  Honor feelings.
- ○ **MENTAL**
  Read or learn.

....
....
....
....
....

EVENING REFLECTIONS

Spread love everywhere you go. Let no one ever come to you without leaving happier. —Mother Teresa

💗 GRATITUDE CHECK

TONIGHT I AM GRATEFUL FOR . . .

1. ....

2. ....

3. ....

Wellness Check

○ WORKOUT   ○ NATURE

○ MEDITATION CAFFEINE: ....

○ NUTRITION   STEPS: ....

WATER INTAKE:

🧠 MENTAL HEALTH CHECK

RIGHT NOW I FEEL . . . (YOU MAY CHOOSE MORE THAN ONE)

○ HAPPY	○ PEACEFUL	○ PROUD
○ LOVING	○ CREATIVE	○ SAD
○ HOPEFUL	○ STRESSED	○ TIRED
○ CALM	○ ANNOYED	○ SCARED
○ ANGRY	○ POSITIVE	○ JOYFUL
○ OVERWHELMED	○ ANXIOUS	○ ....

WHAT IS A MEMORY THAT ALWAYS MAKES YOU SMILE?

....

....

....

....

🏆 WINS FOR THE DAY

TODAY I ACCOMPLISHED . . .

....

....

....

....

💭 MY THOUGHTS & NOTES

....

....

....

....

....

The best and most beautiful things in the world cannot be seen or even touched—they must be felt with the heart. —Helen Keller

---

I FEEL . . . 😄 😍 😴 🙁 😟 😣   I WANT TO FEEL ....

🌹 GRATITUDE CHECK

TODAY I AM GRATEFUL FOR . . .

1. ....

2. ....

3. ....

BE CONSCIOUS OF YOUR REACTIONS AND HOW THEY MAKE YOU FEEL. WHEN YOU ARE AWARE OF YOUR BEHAVIORS YOU CAN STAY POSITIVE.

💡 DAILY AFFIRMATIONS

1. ....

2. ....

3. ....

BONUS: *Read each affirmation 10x in the mirror & throughout the day for faster results.*

☀ 3 PRIORITY GOALS

1. ....

2. ....

3. ....

Self-Care Check

○ **PHYSICAL**
Move or rest.

○ **SOCIAL**
Quality conversation.

○ **SPIRITUAL**
Good for the soul.

○ **HOUSEHOLD**
Cleaning or organizing.

○ **PAMPERING**
Treat yourself.

○ **PERSONAL**
Time on a hobby.

○ **EMOTIONAL**
Honor feelings.

○ **MENTAL**
Read or learn.

💭 MY THOUGHTS & NOTES

....

....

....

....

....

The light that illuminates the world also shines within you. Shine on!

🫀 GRATITUDE CHECK

TONIGHT I AM GRATEFUL FOR . . .

1. ....

2. ....

3. ....

Wellness Check

○ WORKOUT ○ NATURE

○ MEDITATION CAFFEINE: ....

○ NUTRITION STEPS: ....

WATER INTAKE:

🧠 MENTAL HEALTH CHECK

RIGHT NOW I FEEL . . . (YOU MAY CHOOSE MORE THAN ONE)

○ HAPPY	○ PEACEFUL	○ PROUD
○ LOVING	○ CREATIVE	○ SAD
○ HOPEFUL	○ STRESSED	○ TIRED
○ CALM	○ ANNOYED	○ SCARED
○ ANGRY	○ POSITIVE	○ JOYFUL
○ OVERWHELMED	○ ANXIOUS	○ ....

ANSWER THIS: "TOMORROW, I'M FINALLY GOING TO _____."

....

....

....

🏆 WINS FOR THE DAY

TODAY I ACCOMPLISHED . . .

....

....

....

....

💭 MY THOUGHTS & NOTES

....

....

....

....

....

Do good and good will come to you. Happiness is like a boomerang.

I FEEL . . . 😄 😍 😐 😣 😟 😫   I WANT TO FEEL ....

❤ GRATITUDE CHECK

TODAY I AM GRATEFUL FOR . . .

1. ....
2. ....
3. ....

**SEE A POSITIVE INTENT
WITH ADVICE AND
CRITICISM. IT'S EASY TO
THINK SOMEONE IS JUST
TEARING YOU DOWN
WHEN THEY MIGHT BE
TRYING TO BUILD YOU UP.**

💡 DAILY AFFIRMATIONS

1. ....
2. ....
3. ....

BONUS: *Read each affirmation 10x in the mirror & throughout the day for faster results.*

☀ 3 PRIORITY GOALS

1. ....
2. ....
3. ....

Self-Care Check

○ **PHYSICAL**
Move or rest.

○ **SOCIAL**
Quality conversation.

○ **SPIRITUAL**
Good for the soul.

○ **HOUSEHOLD**
Cleaning or organizing.

○ **PAMPERING**
Treat yourself.

○ **PERSONAL**
Time on a hobby.

○ **EMOTIONAL**
Honor feelings.

○ **MENTAL**
Read or learn.

💭 MY THOUGHTS & NOTES

....
....
....
....

It is during our darkest moments that we must focus to see the light.
—Aristotle

♡ GRATITUDE CHECK

TONIGHT I AM GRATEFUL FOR . . .

1. ....

2. ....

3. ....

Wellness Check

○ WORKOUT   ○ NATURE
○ MEDITATION   CAFFEINE: ....
○ NUTRITION   STEPS: ....

WATER INTAKE:

🧠 MENTAL HEALTH CHECK

RIGHT NOW I FEEL . . . (YOU MAY CHOOSE MORE THAN ONE)

○ HAPPY	○ PEACEFUL	○ PROUD
○ LOVING	○ CREATIVE	○ SAD
○ HOPEFUL	○ STRESSED	○ TIRED
○ CALM	○ ANNOYED	○ SCARED
○ ANGRY	○ POSITIVE	○ JOYFUL
○ OVERWHELMED	○ ANXIOUS	○ ....

WHAT DO YOU VALUE MOST IN
A FRIEND?

....

....

....

🏆 WINS FOR THE DAY

TODAY I ACCOMPLISHED . . .

....

....

....

💭 MY THOUGHTS & NOTES

....

....

....

....

....

Living a happy life is not about being a perfect human or everything going just right. You are human, embrace the ups and downs.

I FEEL . . . 😄 😍 😴 🙁 😟 😣   I WANT TO FEEL ....

🫶 GRATITUDE CHECK

TODAY I AM GRATEFUL FOR . . .

1. ....

2. ....

3. ....

**DON'T BE AFRAID TO
TAKE ACTION FIRST.
YOU CAN CONTROL YOUR
OWN DESTINY WHEN
YOU ARE PROACTIVE IN A
POSITIVE WAY.**

💡 DAILY AFFIRMATIONS

1. ....

2. ....

3. ....

BONUS: *Read each affirmation 10x in the mirror & throughout the day for faster results.*

☀️ 3 PRIORITY GOALS

1. ....

2. ....

3. ....

☁️ MY THOUGHTS & NOTES

Self-Care Check

○ **PHYSICAL**
Move or rest.

○ **SOCIAL**
Quality conversation.

○ **SPIRITUAL**
Good for the soul.

○ **HOUSEHOLD**
Cleaning or organizing.

○ **PAMPERING**
Treat yourself.

○ **PERSONAL**
Time on a hobby.

○ **EMOTIONAL**
Honor feelings.

○ **MENTAL**
Read or learn.

....
....
....
....
....

Never let the fear of striking out keep you from playing the game.
—Babe Ruth

GRATITUDE CHECK

TONIGHT I AM GRATEFUL FOR . . .

1. ....

2. ....

3. ....

Wellness Check

- ○ **WORKOUT**   ○ **NATURE**
- ○ **MEDITATION**   **CAFFEINE:** ....
- ○ **NUTRITION**   **STEPS:** ....

WATER INTAKE:

MENTAL HEALTH CHECK

RIGHT NOW I FEEL . . . (YOU MAY CHOOSE MORE THAN ONE)

○ HAPPY	○ PEACEFUL	○ PROUD
○ LOVING	○ CREATIVE	○ SAD
○ HOPEFUL	○ STRESSED	○ TIRED
○ CALM	○ ANNOYED	○ SCARED
○ ANGRY	○ POSITIVE	○ JOYFUL
○ OVERWHELMED	○ ANXIOUS	○ ....

WHAT ARE YOUR CORE VALUES?
ARE YOU LIVING THEM?

....

....

....

WINS FOR THE DAY

TODAY I ACCOMPLISHED . . .

....

....

....

....

MY THOUGHTS & NOTES

....

....

....

....

....

Shine freely, so that every room you enter becomes brighter.

I FEEL . . . 😀 😍 😔 🙁 😢 😣   I WANT TO FEEL ....

🫶 GRATITUDE CHECK

TODAY I AM GRATEFUL FOR . . .

1. ....

2. ....

3. ....

**THINK OF 3 THINGS YOU
CAN DO TO BRING FUN
INTO YOUR DAY . . . GO!**

💡 DAILY AFFIRMATIONS

1. ....

2. ....

3. ....

BONUS: *Read each affirmation 10x in the mirror & throughout the day for faster results.*

☆ 3 PRIORITY GOALS

1. ....

2. ....

3. ....

Self-Care Check

○ **PHYSICAL**
Move or rest.

○ **SOCIAL**
Quality conversation.

○ **SPIRITUAL**
Good for the soul.

○ **HOUSEHOLD**
Cleaning or organizing.

○ **PAMPERING**
Treat yourself.

○ **PERSONAL**
Time on a hobby.

○ **EMOTIONAL**
Honor feelings.

○ **MENTAL**
Read or learn.

☁ MY THOUGHTS & NOTES

....

....

....

....

....

Keep smiling, because life is a beautiful thing and there's so much to smile about. —Marilyn Monroe

---

♡ GRATITUDE CHECK

TONIGHT I AM GRATEFUL FOR . . .

1. ....
2. ....
3. ....

🧠 MENTAL HEALTH CHECK

RIGHT NOW I FEEL . . . (YOU MAY CHOOSE MORE THAN ONE)

○ HAPPY	○ PEACEFUL	○ PROUD
○ LOVING	○ CREATIVE	○ SAD
○ HOPEFUL	○ STRESSED	○ TIRED
○ CALM	○ ANNOYED	○ SCARED
○ ANGRY	○ POSITIVE	○ JOYFUL
○ OVERWHELMED	○ ANXIOUS	○ ....

Wellness Check

○ WORKOUT ○ NATURE
○ MEDITATION CAFFEINE: ....
○ NUTRITION STEPS: ....

WATER INTAKE:

HOW DO YOU REST AND RECHARGE?

....
....
....

🏆 WINS FOR THE DAY

TODAY I ACCOMPLISHED . . .

....
....
....
....

💭 MY THOUGHTS & NOTES

....
....
....
....
....

MORNING INTENTIONS

Whatever the mind of man can conceive and believe, it can achieve.
—Napoleon Hill

I FEEL . . . 😄 😍 😑 🙁 😣 😖   I WANT TO FEEL ....

♡ GRATITUDE CHECK

TODAY I AM GRATEFUL FOR . . .

1. ....

2. ....

3. ....

**FEELING DOWN AND CAN'T
SEEM TO SHAKE IT OFF?
GIVE YOURSELF TIME TO
PROCESS YOUR EMOTIONS
TODAY!**

☀ DAILY AFFIRMATIONS

1. ....

2. ....

3. ....

BONUS: *Read each affirmation 10x in the mirror & throughout the day for faster results.*

☆ 3 PRIORITY GOALS

1. ....

2. ....

3. ....

Self-Care Check

○ **PHYSICAL**   ○ **SOCIAL**
Move or rest.   Quality conversation.

○ **SPIRITUAL**   ○ **HOUSEHOLD**
Good for the soul.   Cleaning or organizing.

○ **PAMPERING**   ○ **PERSONAL**
Treat yourself.   Time on a hobby.

○ **EMOTIONAL**   ○ **MENTAL**
Honor feelings.   Read or learn.

☁ MY THOUGHTS & NOTES

....

....

....

....

....

Note to self: You are worthy and enough. It's time to be happy.

❤️ GRATITUDE CHECK

TONIGHT I AM GRATEFUL FOR . . .

1. ....

2. ....

3. ....

🧠 MENTAL HEALTH CHECK

RIGHT NOW I FEEL . . . (YOU MAY CHOOSE MORE THAN ONE)

○ HAPPY	○ PEACEFUL	○ PROUD
○ LOVING	○ CREATIVE	○ SAD
○ HOPEFUL	○ STRESSED	○ TIRED
○ CALM	○ ANNOYED	○ SCARED
○ ANGRY	○ POSITIVE	○ JOYFUL
○ OVERWHELMED	○ ANXIOUS	○ ....

Wellness Check

○ WORKOUT   ○ NATURE

○ MEDITATION   CAFFEINE: ....

○ NUTRITION   STEPS: ....

WATER INTAKE:

🥛 🥛 🥛 🥛 🥛 🥛 🥛 🥛

WHAT DID YOU DO WITH YOUR FREE TIME TODAY?

....

....

....

....

🏆 WINS FOR THE DAY

TODAY I ACCOMPLISHED . . .

....

....

....

....

💭 MY THOUGHTS & NOTES

....

....

....

....

....

....

A compliment is verbal sunshine. —Robert Orben

_____

I FEEL . . . 😄 😍 😴 🙁 😣 😒   I WANT TO FEEL ....

🌿 GRATITUDE CHECK

TODAY I AM GRATEFUL FOR . . .

1. ....

2. ....

3. ....

PRIORITIZE THIS QUESTION TODAY WITH YOURSELF AND FRIENDS OR CO-WORKERS: "WHAT IS GOING RIGHT?"

💡 DAILY AFFIRMATIONS

1. ....

2. ....

3. ....

BONUS: *Read each affirmation 10x in the mirror & throughout the day for faster results.*

☀ 3 PRIORITY GOALS

1. ....

2. ....

3. ....

☁ MY THOUGHTS & NOTES

Self-Care Check

○ **PHYSICAL**
Move or rest.

○ **SOCIAL**
Quality conversation.

○ **SPIRITUAL**
Good for the soul.

○ **HOUSEHOLD**
Cleaning or organizing.

○ **PAMPERING**
Treat yourself.

○ **PERSONAL**
Time on a hobby.

○ **EMOTIONAL**
Honor feelings.

○ **MENTAL**
Read or learn.

....

....

....

....

EVENING REFLECTIONS

It makes a big difference in your life when you stay positive.

❤ GRATITUDE CHECK

TONIGHT I AM GRATEFUL FOR . . .

1. ....
2. ....
3. ....

🧠 MENTAL HEALTH CHECK

RIGHT NOW I FEEL . . . (YOU MAY CHOOSE MORE THAN ONE)

O HAPPY	O PEACEFUL	O PROUD
O LOVING	O CREATIVE	O SAD
O HOPEFUL	O STRESSED	O TIRED
O CALM	O ANNOYED	O SCARED
O ANGRY	O POSITIVE	O JOYFUL
O OVERWHELMED	O ANXIOUS	O ....

Wellness Check

- O WORKOUT   O NATURE
- O MEDITATION CAFFEINE: ....
- O NUTRITION STEPS: ....

WATER INTAKE:

IF YOU WERE TO BE KNOWN FOR SOMETHING, WHAT WOULD THAT BE?

....
....
....

🏆 WINS FOR THE DAY

TODAY I ACCOMPLISHED . . .

....
....
....

💭 MY THOUGHTS & NOTES

....
....
....
....
....

Ask and you shall receive that your joy may be full. —John 16:24

I FEEL . . . 😄 😍 😴 🙁 😟 😣   I WANT TO FEEL ....

🤍 GRATITUDE CHECK

TODAY I AM GRATEFUL FOR . . .

1. ....

2. ....

3. ....

**ANSWER THE QUESTION:
"WHAT DOES HAPPINESS
MEAN TO ME?" HOW
CAN YOU CULTIVATE
THIS TODAY?**

💡 DAILY AFFIRMATIONS

1. ....

2. ....

3. ....

BONUS: *Read each affirmation 10x in the mirror & throughout the day for faster results.*

☆ 3 PRIORITY GOALS

1. ....

2. ....

3. ....

Self-Care Check

- ○ **PHYSICAL**
  Move or rest.
- ○ **SOCIAL**
  Quality conversation.
- ○ **SPIRITUAL**
  Good for the soul.
- ○ **HOUSEHOLD**
  Cleaning or organizing.
- ○ **PAMPERING**
  Treat yourself.
- ○ **PERSONAL**
  Time on a hobby.
- ○ **EMOTIONAL**
  Honor feelings.
- ○ **MENTAL**
  Read or learn.

💭 MY THOUGHTS & NOTES

....

....

....

....

....

EVENING REFLECTIONS

The happiest people in life are the givers, not the receivers.

🌹 GRATITUDE CHECK

TONIGHT I AM GRATEFUL FOR . . .

1. ....

2. ....

3. ....

Wellness Check

○ WORKOUT ○ NATURE

○ MEDITATION CAFFEINE: ....

○ NUTRITION STEPS: ....

WATER INTAKE:

🧠 MENTAL HEALTH CHECK

RIGHT NOW I FEEL . . . (YOU MAY CHOOSE MORE THAN ONE)

○ HAPPY	○ PEACEFUL	○ PROUD
○ LOVING	○ CREATIVE	○ SAD
○ HOPEFUL	○ STRESSED	○ TIRED
○ CALM	○ ANNOYED	○ SCARED
○ ANGRY	○ POSITIVE	○ JOYFUL
○ OVERWHELMED	○ ANXIOUS	○ ....

WHAT TOPICS DO YOU FEEL LIKE
AN EXPERT ON?

....

....

....

🏆 WINS FOR THE DAY

TODAY I ACCOMPLISHED . . .

....

....

....

....

💭 MY THOUGHTS & NOTES

....

....

....

....

....

The more you enjoy your life, the more life gives you things to enjoy.

I FEEL . . . 😄 😍 😴 🙁 😣 😖   I WANT TO FEEL ....

❤️ GRATITUDE CHECK

TODAY I AM GRATEFUL FOR . . .

1. ....

2. ....

3. ....

SIT WITH A FRIEND AND PING PONG BACK AND FORTH GRATITUDE STATEMENTS FOR FIVE MINUTES.

💡 DAILY AFFIRMATIONS

1. ....

2. ....

3. ....

BONUS: *Read each affirmation 10x in the mirror & throughout the day for faster results.*

☀️ 3 PRIORITY GOALS

1. ....

2. ....

3. ....

💭 MY THOUGHTS & NOTES

Self-Care Check

○ **PHYSICAL**
Move or rest.

○ **SOCIAL**
Quality conversation.

○ **SPIRITUAL**
Good for the soul.

○ **HOUSEHOLD**
Cleaning or organizing.

○ **PAMPERING**
Treat yourself.

○ **PERSONAL**
Time on a hobby.

○ **EMOTIONAL**
Honor feelings.

○ **MENTAL**
Read or learn.

....

....

....

....

....

One day, you will realize that it had to happen, in that way, to give you the lessons you needed to grow. —Vex King

---

🌸 GRATITUDE CHECK

TONIGHT I AM GRATEFUL FOR . . .

1. ....
2. ....
3. ....

Wellness Check

○ **WORKOUT**   ○ **NATURE**
○ **MEDITATION**   CAFFEINE: ....
○ **NUTRITION**   STEPS: ....

WATER INTAKE:

🧠 MENTAL HEALTH CHECK

RIGHT NOW I FEEL . . . (YOU MAY CHOOSE MORE THAN ONE)

○ HAPPY	○ PEACEFUL	○ PROUD
○ LOVING	○ CREATIVE	○ SAD
○ HOPEFUL	○ STRESSED	○ TIRED
○ CALM	○ ANNOYED	○ SCARED
○ ANGRY	○ POSITIVE	○ JOYFUL
○ OVERWHELMED	○ ANXIOUS	○ ....

WHAT ARE SOME WAYS YOU WOULD LIKE TO SERVE YOUR COMMUNITY?

....
....
....

🏆 WINS FOR THE DAY

TODAY I ACCOMPLISHED . . .

....
....
....

💭 MY THOUGHTS & NOTES

....
....
....
....
....

Work hard, play hard, dream big, and believe in yourself.

I FEEL . . . 😆 😍 😴 🙁 😟 😣   I WANT TO FEEL ....

❤️ GRATITUDE CHECK

TODAY I AM GRATEFUL FOR . . .

1. ....

2. ....

3. ....

THANK TWO FRIENDS WHO HAVE HAD A POSITIVE IMPACT ON YOUR LIFE TODAY. JOURNAL WHAT HAPPENED!

💡 DAILY AFFIRMATIONS

1. ....

2. ....

3. ....

BONUS: *Read each affirmation 10x in the mirror & throughout the day for faster results.*

⭐ 3 PRIORITY GOALS

1. ....

2. ....

3. ....

💭 MY THOUGHTS & NOTES

Self-Care Check

○ **PHYSICAL**
Move or rest.

○ **SOCIAL**
Quality conversation.

○ **SPIRITUAL**
Good for the soul.

○ **HOUSEHOLD**
Cleaning or organizing.

○ **PAMPERING**
Treat yourself.

○ **PERSONAL**
Time on a hobby.

○ **EMOTIONAL**
Honor feelings.

○ **MENTAL**
Read or learn.

....

....

....

....

Do not let making a living prevent you from making a life.
—John Wooden

🫀 GRATITUDE CHECK

TONIGHT I AM GRATEFUL FOR . . .

1. ....

2. ....

3. ....

Wellness Check

○ **WORKOUT**   ○ **NATURE**

○ **MEDITATION** CAFFEINE: ....

○ **NUTRITION**   STEPS: ....

WATER INTAKE:

🧠 MENTAL HEALTH CHECK

RIGHT NOW I FEEL . . . (YOU MAY CHOOSE MORE THAN ONE)

○ HAPPY	○ PEACEFUL	○ PROUD
○ LOVING	○ CREATIVE	○ SAD
○ HOPEFUL	○ STRESSED	○ TIRED
○ CALM	○ ANNOYED	○ SCARED
○ ANGRY	○ POSITIVE	○ JOYFUL
○ OVERWHELMED	○ ANXIOUS	○ ....

ANSWER THIS: "I'M PROUD OF THE WAY I _____ TODAY."

....

....

....

🏆 WINS FOR THE DAY

TODAY I ACCOMPLISHED . . .

....

....

....

....

💭 MY THOUGHTS & NOTES

....

....

....

....

....

Joy expands your life. Prioritize joy each day and watch your life transform.

I FEEL . . . 😄 😍 😑 🙁 ☹️ 😣   I WANT TO FEEL ....

🧠 GRATITUDE CHECK

TODAY I AM GRATEFUL FOR . . .

1. ....

2. ....

3. ....

THINK OF SOMETHING A HAPPY PERSON WOULD DO, AND DO IT. JOURNAL ABOUT IT THIS EVENING!

💡 DAILY AFFIRMATIONS

1. ....

2. ....

3. ....

BONUS: *Read each affirmation 10x in the mirror & throughout the day for faster results.*

☀️ 3 PRIORITY GOALS

1. ....

2. ....

3. ....

Self-Care Check

○ **PHYSICAL**
Move or rest.

○ **SOCIAL**
Quality conversation.

○ **SPIRITUAL**
Good for the soul.

○ **HOUSEHOLD**
Cleaning or organizing.

○ **PAMPERING**
Treat yourself.

○ **PERSONAL**
Time on a hobby.

○ **EMOTIONAL**
Honor feelings.

○ **MENTAL**
Read or learn.

💭 MY THOUGHTS & NOTES

....

....

....

....

....

Ask yourself: "Do I want to be happy or do I want to be right?" Then let go of any thought that's keeping you from being happy.

🌹 GRATITUDE CHECK

TONIGHT I AM GRATEFUL FOR . . .

1. ....

2. ....

3. ....

🧠 MENTAL HEALTH CHECK

RIGHT NOW I FEEL . . . (YOU MAY CHOOSE MORE THAN ONE)

○ HAPPY	○ PEACEFUL	○ PROUD
○ LOVING	○ CREATIVE	○ SAD
○ HOPEFUL	○ STRESSED	○ TIRED
○ CALM	○ ANNOYED	○ SCARED
○ ANGRY	○ POSITIVE	○ JOYFUL
○ OVERWHELMED	○ ANXIOUS	○ ....

Wellness Check

○ WORKOUT ○ NATURE
○ MEDITATION CAFFEINE: ....
○ NUTRITION STEPS: ....

WATER INTAKE:

🥛 🥛 🥛 🥛 🥛 🥛 🥛

WHAT'S THE SCARIEST THING YOU'VE EVER DONE THAT TURNED OUT TO BE WORTH IT?

....

....

....

🏆 WINS FOR THE DAY

TODAY I ACCOMPLISHED . . .

....

....

....

....

💭 MY THOUGHTS & NOTES

....

....

....

....

....

....

Happiness is not a destination. It's available right now. Seek it. Feel it.

_____

I FEEL . . . 😄 😍 😑 🙁 😢 😣   I WANT TO FEEL ....

❤ GRATITUDE CHECK

TODAY I AM GRATEFUL FOR . . .

1. ....

2. ....

3. ....

CLEAN YOUR ROOM OR LIVING SPACE. DECLUTTERING ALSO HELPS WITH ANXIETY, OVERTHINKING, AND RUMINATING THOUGHTS.

💡 DAILY AFFIRMATIONS

1. ....

2. ....

3. ....

BONUS: *Read each affirmation 10x in the mirror & throughout the day for faster results.*

☀ 3 PRIORITY GOALS

1. ....

2. ....

3. ....

☁ MY THOUGHTS & NOTES

Self-Care Check

○ **PHYSICAL**
Move or rest.

○ **SOCIAL**
Quality conversation.

○ **SPIRITUAL**
Good for the soul.

○ **HOUSEHOLD**
Cleaning or organizing.

○ **PAMPERING**
Treat yourself.

○ **PERSONAL**
Time on a hobby.

○ **EMOTIONAL**
Honor feelings.

○ **MENTAL**
Read or learn.

....

....

....

....

....

EVENING REFLECTIONS

DATE: .... / .... / ....

Dreaming, after all, is a form of planning. —Gloria Steinem

🌸 GRATITUDE CHECK

TONIGHT I AM GRATEFUL FOR . . .

1. ....

2. ....

3. ....

Wellness Check

○ WORKOUT   ○ NATURE

○ MEDITATION CAFFEINE: ....

○ NUTRITION   STEPS: ....

WATER INTAKE:

🧠 MENTAL HEALTH CHECK

RIGHT NOW I FEEL . . . (YOU MAY CHOOSE MORE THAN ONE)

○ HAPPY	○ PEACEFUL	○ PROUD
○ LOVING	○ CREATIVE	○ SAD
○ HOPEFUL	○ STRESSED	○ TIRED
○ CALM	○ ANNOYED	○ SCARED
○ ANGRY	○ POSITIVE	○ JOYFUL
○ OVERWHELMED	○ ANXIOUS	○ ....

WHAT KIND OF RANDOM ACT OF KINDNESS COULD YOU DO TOMORROW?

....

....

....

🏆 WINS FOR THE DAY

TODAY I ACCOMPLISHED . . .

....

....

....

💭 MY THOUGHTS & NOTES

....

....

....

....

....

You stop judging others when you stop judging yourself.

I FEEL . . . 😀 😍 😴 🙁 😣 😖   I WANT TO FEEL ....

🌋 GRATITUDE CHECK

TODAY I AM GRATEFUL FOR . . .

1. ....

2. ....

3. ....

MAKE A LIST OF EVERYTHING YOU LOVE ABOUT YOURSELF. WHAT IS ONE WAY YOU CAN THANK YOURSELF FOR ALL THESE WONDERFUL GIFTS?

💡 DAILY AFFIRMATIONS

1. ....

2. ....

3. ....

BONUS: *Read each affirmation 10x in the mirror & throughout the day for faster results.*

☀ 3 PRIORITY GOALS

1. ....

2. ....

3. ....

Self-Care Check

- O **PHYSICAL** Move or rest.
- O **SOCIAL** Quality conversation.
- O **SPIRITUAL** Good for the soul.
- O **HOUSEHOLD** Cleaning or organizing.
- O **PAMPERING** Treat yourself.
- O **PERSONAL** Time on a hobby.
- O **EMOTIONAL** Honor feelings.
- O **MENTAL** Read or learn.

💭 MY THOUGHTS & NOTES

....

....

....

....

....

Stop trying to prove your worth. You're worthy because you exist.

♡ GRATITUDE CHECK

TONIGHT I AM GRATEFUL FOR . . .

1. ....
2. ....
3. ....

🧠 MENTAL HEALTH CHECK

RIGHT NOW I FEEL . . . (YOU MAY CHOOSE MORE THAN ONE)

○ HAPPY	○ PEACEFUL	○ PROUD
○ LOVING	○ CREATIVE	○ SAD
○ HOPEFUL	○ STRESSED	○ TIRED
○ CALM	○ ANNOYED	○ SCARED
○ ANGRY	○ POSITIVE	○ JOYFUL
○ OVERWHELMED	○ ANXIOUS	○ ....

Wellness Check

○ WORKOUT   ○ NATURE
○ MEDITATION   CAFFEINE: ....
○ NUTRITION   STEPS: ....

WATER INTAKE:

IF YOU COULD GIVE ANYONE A PIECE OF ADVICE TO GET THROUGH THEIR DAY, WHAT WOULD IT BE?

....
....
....

🏆 WINS FOR THE DAY

TODAY I ACCOMPLISHED . . .

....
....
....
....

💭 MY THOUGHTS & NOTES

....
....
....
....
....

Having a positive mindset means prioritizing mental habits that make you feel better.

I FEEL . . . 😄 😍 😑 🙁 😣 😫   I WANT TO FEEL ....

❤️ GRATITUDE CHECK

TODAY I AM GRATEFUL FOR . . .

1. ....

2. ....

3. ....

FIND A WAY TO SPEND SOME OR MORE TIME WITH ANIMALS TODAY. ANIMALS EXPAND THE HEART!

💡 DAILY AFFIRMATIONS

1. ....

2. ....

3. ....

BONUS: *Read each affirmation 10x in the mirror & throughout the day for faster results.*

☀️ 3 PRIORITY GOALS

1. ....

2. ....

3. ....

💭 MY THOUGHTS & NOTES

Self-Care Check

○ **PHYSICAL**
Move or rest.

○ **SOCIAL**
Quality conversation.

○ **SPIRITUAL**
Good for the soul.

○ **HOUSEHOLD**
Cleaning or organizing.

○ **PAMPERING**
Treat yourself.

○ **PERSONAL**
Time on a hobby.

○ **EMOTIONAL**
Honor feelings.

○ **MENTAL**
Read or learn.

....
....
....
....

Fill your mind with positive thoughts, and you'll fill your life with blessings.

GRATITUDE CHECK

TONIGHT I AM GRATEFUL FOR . . .

1. ....
2. ....
3. ....

Wellness Check

- ○ WORKOUT   ○ NATURE
- ○ MEDITATION   CAFFEINE: ....
- ○ NUTRITION   STEPS: ....

WATER INTAKE:

MENTAL HEALTH CHECK

RIGHT NOW I FEEL . . . (YOU MAY CHOOSE MORE THAN ONE)

- ○ HAPPY
- ○ LOVING
- ○ HOPEFUL
- ○ CALM
- ○ ANGRY
- ○ OVERWHELMED

- ○ PEACEFUL
- ○ CREATIVE
- ○ STRESSED
- ○ ANNOYED
- ○ POSITIVE
- ○ ANXIOUS

- ○ PROUD
- ○ SAD
- ○ TIRED
- ○ SCARED
- ○ JOYFUL
- ○ ....

IF YOU HAD A MAGIC WAND, WHAT WOULD YOU WISH FOR RIGHT NOW?

....
....
....

WINS FOR THE DAY

TODAY I ACCOMPLISHED . . .

....
....
....
....

MY THOUGHTS & NOTES

....
....
....
....
....

Whether you think you can or whether you think you can't—either way, you're right. —Henry Ford

---

I FEEL . . . 😄 😍 😌 🙁 😞 😖   I WANT TO FEEL ....

💗 GRATITUDE CHECK

TODAY I AM GRATEFUL FOR . . .

1. ....

2. ....

3. ....

**TODAY, CALL SOMEONE
YOU LOVE BUT HAVE NOT
CHECKED ON IN A WHILE.
TELL THEM HOW MUCH
YOU CARE!**

💡 DAILY AFFIRMATIONS

1. ....

2. ....

3. ....

BONUS: *Read each affirmation 10x in the mirror & throughout the day for faster results.*

☆ 3 PRIORITY GOALS

1. ....

2. ....

3. ....

Self-Care Check

- ○ **PHYSICAL**
  Move or rest.
- ○ **SOCIAL**
  Quality conversation.
- ○ **SPIRITUAL**
  Good for the soul.
- ○ **HOUSEHOLD**
  Cleaning or organizing.
- ○ **PAMPERING**
  Treat yourself.
- ○ **PERSONAL**
  Time on a hobby.
- ○ **EMOTIONAL**
  Honor feelings.
- ○ **MENTAL**
  Read or learn.

💭 MY THOUGHTS & NOTES

....

....

....

....

....

Ignore what upsets you. Amplify what brings you joy.

🌹 GRATITUDE CHECK

TONIGHT I AM GRATEFUL FOR . . .

1. ....

2. ....

3. ....

Wellness Check

- ○ WORKOUT   ○ NATURE
- ○ MEDITATION   CAFFEINE: ....
- ○ NUTRITION   STEPS: ....

WATER INTAKE:

🥛 🥛 🥛 🥛 🥛 🥛 🥛

🧠 MENTAL HEALTH CHECK

RIGHT NOW I FEEL . . . (YOU MAY CHOOSE MORE THAN ONE)

○ HAPPY	○ PEACEFUL	○ PROUD
○ LOVING	○ CREATIVE	○ SAD
○ HOPEFUL	○ STRESSED	○ TIRED
○ CALM	○ ANNOYED	○ SCARED
○ ANGRY	○ POSITIVE	○ JOYFUL
○ OVERWHELMED	○ ANXIOUS	○ ....

WHAT PAST MEMORY STILL HURTS? HOW CAN YOU BRING FORGIVENESS OR LIGHT?

....

....

....

🏆 WINS FOR THE DAY

TODAY I ACCOMPLISHED . . .

....

....

....

....

💭 MY THOUGHTS & NOTES

....

....

....

....

....

....

Perhaps the greatest gift anyone can give to their children is teaching them to see the positive things in their daily life.

I FEEL . . . 😄 😍 😴 🙁 😟 😣   I WANT TO FEEL ....

❤️ GRATITUDE CHECK

TODAY I AM GRATEFUL FOR . . .

1. ....

2. ....

3. ....

THINK ABOUT YOUR FAVORITE DISH. NOW PLAN TO COOK IT FOR YOURSELF, AND ENJOY IT.

🌟 DAILY AFFIRMATIONS

1. ....

2. ....

3. ....

BONUS: *Read each affirmation 10x in the mirror & throughout the day for faster results.*

☆ 3 PRIORITY GOALS

1. ....

2. ....

3. ....

☁️ MY THOUGHTS & NOTES

Self-Care Check

○ **PHYSICAL**
Move or rest.

○ **SOCIAL**
Quality conversation.

○ **SPIRITUAL**
Good for the soul.

○ **HOUSEHOLD**
Cleaning or organizing.

○ **PAMPERING**
Treat yourself.

○ **PERSONAL**
Time on a hobby.

○ **EMOTIONAL**
Honor feelings.

○ **MENTAL**
Read or learn.

....

....

....

....

....

The most interesting people are the most interested people.

🌱 GRATITUDE CHECK

TONIGHT I AM GRATEFUL FOR . . .

1. ....
2. ....
3. ....

Wellness Check

○ WORKOUT   ○ NATURE
○ MEDITATION   CAFFEINE: ....
○ NUTRITION   STEPS: ....

WATER INTAKE:

🧠 MENTAL HEALTH CHECK

RIGHT NOW I FEEL . . . (YOU MAY CHOOSE MORE THAN ONE)

○ HAPPY	○ PEACEFUL	○ PROUD
○ LOVING	○ CREATIVE	○ SAD
○ HOPEFUL	○ STRESSED	○ TIRED
○ CALM	○ ANNOYED	○ SCARED
○ ANGRY	○ POSITIVE	○ JOYFUL
○ OVERWHELMED	○ ANXIOUS	○ ....

LIST 3 FAMILY MEMBERS YOU ARE MOST GRATEFUL FOR . . .

....

....

....

🏆 WINS FOR THE DAY

TODAY I ACCOMPLISHED . . .

....

....

....

....

💭 MY THOUGHTS & NOTES

....

....

....

....

....

....

If you want to create, you must give yourself space to play and dwell in the possibilities.

I FEEL . . . 😄 😍 😴 🙁 😣 😖   I WANT TO FEEL ....

❤ GRATITUDE CHECK

TODAY I AM GRATEFUL FOR . . .

1. ....

2. ....

3. ....

PUT ON AN OUTFIT THAT MAKES YOU FEEL CONFIDENT. WEAR IT PROUDLY TODAY!

💡 DAILY AFFIRMATIONS

1. ....

2. ....

3. ....

BONUS: *Read each affirmation 10x in the mirror & throughout the day for faster results.*

☀ 3 PRIORITY GOALS

1. ....

2. ....

3. ....

💭 MY THOUGHTS & NOTES

Self-Care Check

- ○ **PHYSICAL**
  Move or rest.
- ○ **SOCIAL**
  Quality conversation.
- ○ **SPIRITUAL**
  Good for the soul.
- ○ **HOUSEHOLD**
  Cleaning or organizing.
- ○ **PAMPERING**
  Treat yourself.
- ○ **PERSONAL**
  Time on a hobby.
- ○ **EMOTIONAL**
  Honor feelings.
- ○ **MENTAL**
  Read or learn.

....

....

....

....

....

EVENING REFLECTIONS

Be here right now, because the real you is accessed only in the present moment.

❤️ GRATITUDE CHECK

TONIGHT I AM GRATEFUL FOR . . .

1. ....

2. ....

3. ....

Wellness Check

- ○ WORKOUT   ○ NATURE
- ○ MEDITATION CAFFEINE: ....
- ○ NUTRITION   STEPS: ....

WATER INTAKE:

🧠 MENTAL HEALTH CHECK

RIGHT NOW I FEEL . . . (YOU MAY CHOOSE MORE THAN ONE)

○ HAPPY	○ PEACEFUL	○ PROUD
○ LOVING	○ CREATIVE	○ SAD
○ HOPEFUL	○ STRESSED	○ TIRED
○ CALM	○ ANNOYED	○ SCARED
○ ANGRY	○ POSITIVE	○ JOYFUL
○ OVERWHELMED	○ ANXIOUS	○ ....

WHAT ARE YOU MOST PASSIONATE ABOUT RIGHT NOW?

....

....

....

🏆 WINS FOR THE DAY

TODAY I ACCOMPLISHED . . .

....

....

....

....

💭 MY THOUGHTS & NOTES

....

....

....

....

....

....

Sometimes all you can do is just trust, letting go of the fear of the unknown.

I FEEL . . . 😄 😍 😴 🙁 😢 😣   I WANT TO FEEL ....

♡ GRATITUDE CHECK

TODAY I AM GRATEFUL FOR . . .

1. ....

2. ....

3. ....

**PLAY YOUR FAVORITE
SONG AND DANCE TODAY.
BONUS IF YOU DO IT
WITH OTHERS.**

☼♡ DAILY AFFIRMATIONS

1. ....

2. ....

3. ....

BONUS: *Read each affirmation 10x in the mirror & throughout the day for faster results.*

☼ 3 PRIORITY GOALS

1. ....

2. ....

3. ....

☁ MY THOUGHTS & NOTES

Self-Care Check

○ **PHYSICAL**
Move or rest.

○ **SOCIAL**
Quality conversation.

○ **SPIRITUAL**
Good for the soul.

○ **HOUSEHOLD**
Cleaning or organizing.

○ **PAMPERING**
Treat yourself.

○ **PERSONAL**
Time on a hobby.

○ **EMOTIONAL**
Honor feelings.

○ **MENTAL**
Read or learn.

....

....

....

....

....

Live in the present, because this is the only real moment.

♡ GRATITUDE CHECK

TONIGHT I AM GRATEFUL FOR . . .

1. ....
2. ....
3. ....

Wellness Check

○ WORKOUT   ○ NATURE
○ MEDITATION   CAFFEINE: ....
○ NUTRITION   STEPS: ....

WATER INTAKE:

🧠 MENTAL HEALTH CHECK

RIGHT NOW I FEEL . . . (YOU MAY CHOOSE MORE THAN ONE)

○ HAPPY	○ PEACEFUL	○ PROUD
○ LOVING	○ CREATIVE	○ SAD
○ HOPEFUL	○ STRESSED	○ TIRED
○ CALM	○ ANNOYED	○ SCARED
○ ANGRY	○ POSITIVE	○ JOYFUL
○ OVERWHELMED	○ ANXIOUS	○ ....

WHAT CAN YOU DO THIS
WEEKEND TO RECHARGE?

....
....
....

🏆 WINS FOR THE DAY

TODAY I ACCOMPLISHED . . .

....
....
....
....

💭 MY THOUGHTS & NOTES

....
....
....
....
....

You love others more deeply when you love yourself. Fill your cup!

I FEEL . . . 😄 😍 😐 😴 🙁 😣   I WANT TO FEEL ....

♡ GRATITUDE CHECK

TODAY I AM GRATEFUL FOR . . .

1. ....

2. ....

3. ....

☼ DAILY AFFIRMATIONS

1. ....

2. ....

3. ....

BONUS: *Read each affirmation 10x in the mirror & throughout the day for faster results.*

MAKE A LIST OF YOUR BIGGEST SUCCESSES. READ YOUR LIST AS THOUGH YOU'RE READING SOMEONE ELSE'S ACCOMPLISHMENTS, AND ACKNOWLEDGE WHAT AN INCREDIBLE PERSON YOU ARE.

☼ 3 PRIORITY GOALS

1. ....

2. ....

3. ....

☁ MY THOUGHTS & NOTES

Self-Care Check

○ **PHYSICAL**
Move or rest.

○ **SOCIAL**
Quality conversation.

○ **SPIRITUAL**
Good for the soul.

○ **HOUSEHOLD**
Cleaning or organizing.

○ **PAMPERING**
Treat yourself.

○ **PERSONAL**
Time on a hobby.

○ **EMOTIONAL**
Honor feelings.

○ **MENTAL**
Read or learn.

....

....

....

....

Next time you go shopping, remember this: Happiness is free and always in stock.

♡ GRATITUDE CHECK

TONIGHT I AM GRATEFUL FOR . . .

1. ....

2. ....

3. ....

Wellness Check

- ○ WORKOUT
- ○ MEDITATION
- ○ NUTRITION
- ○ NATURE
- CAFFEINE: ....
- STEPS: ....

WATER INTAKE:

🧠 MENTAL HEALTH CHECK

RIGHT NOW I FEEL . . . (YOU MAY CHOOSE MORE THAN ONE)

○ HAPPY	○ PEACEFUL	○ PROUD
○ LOVING	○ CREATIVE	○ SAD
○ HOPEFUL	○ STRESSED	○ TIRED
○ CALM	○ ANNOYED	○ SCARED
○ ANGRY	○ POSITIVE	○ JOYFUL
○ OVERWHELMED	○ ANXIOUS	○ ....

HOW MUCH DO YOU SCROLL SOCIAL MEDIA? IS THERE SOMETHING YOU'D RATHER DO?

....

....

....

🏆 WINS FOR THE DAY

TODAY I ACCOMPLISHED . . .

....

....

....

☁ MY THOUGHTS & NOTES

....

....

....

....

....

Things work out best for those who make the best of how things work out. —John Wooden

I FEEL . . . 😃 😍 😴 🙁 😔 😣   I WANT TO FEEL ....

❤️ GRATITUDE CHECK

TODAY I AM GRATEFUL FOR . . .

1. ....

2. ....

3. ....

DAYDREAM ABOUT SOMETHING YOU WANT. SAY TO YOURSELF, "WOULDN'T IT BE GREAT IF _____" AND LET YOUR IMAGINATION RUN WILD.

💡 DAILY AFFIRMATIONS

1. ....

2. ....

3. ....

BONUS: *Read each affirmation 10x in the mirror & throughout the day for faster results.*

☀️ 3 PRIORITY GOALS

1. ....

2. ....

3. ....

☁️ MY THOUGHTS & NOTES

Self-Care Check

- ○ **PHYSICAL** Move or rest.
- ○ **SOCIAL** Quality conversation.
- ○ **SPIRITUAL** Good for the soul.
- ○ **HOUSEHOLD** Cleaning or organizing.
- ○ **PAMPERING** Treat yourself.
- ○ **PERSONAL** Time on a hobby.
- ○ **EMOTIONAL** Honor feelings.
- ○ **MENTAL** Read or learn.

....

....

....

....

....

Gratitude turns you into a magnet for all the happiness and good that you seek.

♡ GRATITUDE CHECK

TONIGHT I AM GRATEFUL FOR . . .

1. ....

2. ....

3. ....

Wellness Check

○ WORKOUT   ○ NATURE
○ MEDITATION   CAFFEINE: ....
○ NUTRITION   STEPS: ....

WATER INTAKE:

🧠 MENTAL HEALTH CHECK

RIGHT NOW I FEEL . . . (YOU MAY CHOOSE MORE THAN ONE)

○ HAPPY	○ PEACEFUL	○ PROUD
○ LOVING	○ CREATIVE	○ SAD
○ HOPEFUL	○ STRESSED	○ TIRED
○ CALM	○ ANNOYED	○ SCARED
○ ANGRY	○ POSITIVE	○ JOYFUL
○ OVERWHELMED	○ ANXIOUS	○ ....

WHAT DREAM OR GOAL WOULD YOU LIKE TO RE-IGNITE IN YOUR HEART?

....

....

....

🏆 WINS FOR THE DAY

TODAY I ACCOMPLISHED . . .

....

....

....

💭 MY THOUGHTS & NOTES

....

....

....

....

....

Choose to see the best in others and others will see the best in you.

I FEEL . . . 😄 😍 😴 🙁 😣 😖   I WANT TO FEEL ....

❤ GRATITUDE CHECK

TODAY I AM GRATEFUL FOR . . .

1. ....

2. ....

3. ....

**DESCRIBE A GOAL
AS THOUGH YOU'VE
ALREADY ACHIEVED IT,
FEELING ELATED AND
ACCOMPLISHED!**

💡 DAILY AFFIRMATIONS

1. ....

2. ....

3. ....

BONUS: *Read each affirmation 10x in the mirror & throughout the day for faster results.*

☀ 3 PRIORITY GOALS

1. ....

2. ....

3. ....

☁ MY THOUGHTS & NOTES

Self-Care Check

- ○ **PHYSICAL**
  Move or rest.
- ○ **SOCIAL**
  Quality conversation.
- ○ **SPIRITUAL**
  Good for the soul.
- ○ **HOUSEHOLD**
  Cleaning or organizing.
- ○ **PAMPERING**
  Treat yourself.
- ○ **PERSONAL**
  Time on a hobby.
- ○ **EMOTIONAL**
  Honor feelings.
- ○ **MENTAL**
  Read or learn.

....

....

....

....

....

Keep your heart open and allow your capacity for love to expand to others—even strangers.

GRATITUDE CHECK

TONIGHT I AM GRATEFUL FOR . . .

1. ....

2. ....

3. ....

Wellness Check

- ○ WORKOUT   ○ NATURE
- ○ MEDITATION   CAFFEINE: ....
- ○ NUTRITION   STEPS: ....

WATER INTAKE:

MENTAL HEALTH CHECK

RIGHT NOW I FEEL . . . (YOU MAY CHOOSE MORE THAN ONE)

○ HAPPY	○ PEACEFUL	○ PROUD
○ LOVING	○ CREATIVE	○ SAD
○ HOPEFUL	○ STRESSED	○ TIRED
○ CALM	○ ANNOYED	○ SCARED
○ ANGRY	○ POSITIVE	○ JOYFUL
○ OVERWHELMED	○ ANXIOUS	○ ....

WHAT DO YOU VALUE MOST IN YOURSELF?

....

....

....

WINS FOR THE DAY

TODAY I ACCOMPLISHED . . .

....

....

....

....

MY THOUGHTS & NOTES

....

....

....

....

....

MORNING INTENTIONS

Your purpose in life is to enjoy life. Don't wait for blessings.
Be happy right now!

I FEEL . . . 😄 😍 😐 ☹️ 🙁 😣   I WANT TO FEEL ....

🧠 GRATITUDE CHECK

TODAY I AM GRATEFUL FOR . . .

1. ....

2. ....

3. ....

CONJURE UP AN IMAGE OF THE VERSION OF YOU WHO FEELS HAPPY, WORTHY, AND LOVABLE. OBSERVE HOW THIS VERSION OF YOU SHOWS UP!

💡 DAILY AFFIRMATIONS

1. ....

2. ....

3. ....

BONUS: *Read each affirmation 10x in the mirror & throughout the day for faster results.*

☀️ 3 PRIORITY GOALS

1. ....

2. ....

3. ....

Self-Care Check

○ **PHYSICAL**
Move or rest.

○ **SOCIAL**
Quality conversation.

○ **SPIRITUAL**
Good for the soul.

○ **HOUSEHOLD**
Cleaning or organizing.

○ **PAMPERING**
Treat yourself.

○ **PERSONAL**
Time on a hobby.

○ **EMOTIONAL**
Honor feelings.

○ **MENTAL**
Read or learn.

☁️ MY THOUGHTS & NOTES

....

....

....

....

EVENING REFLECTIONS

There's nothing for you to do other than to be. You are already whole.

♡ GRATITUDE CHECK

TONIGHT I AM GRATEFUL FOR . . .

1. ....
2. ....
3. ....

Wellness Check

○ WORKOUT ○ NATURE
○ MEDITATION CAFFEINE: ....
○ NUTRITION STEPS: ....

WATER INTAKE:

🧠 MENTAL HEALTH CHECK

RIGHT NOW I FEEL . . . (YOU MAY CHOOSE MORE THAN ONE)

○ HAPPY	○ PEACEFUL	○ PROUD
○ LOVING	○ CREATIVE	○ SAD
○ HOPEFUL	○ STRESSED	○ TIRED
○ CALM	○ ANNOYED	○ SCARED
○ ANGRY	○ POSITIVE	○ JOYFUL
○ OVERWHELMED	○ ANXIOUS	○ ....

WHAT SELF CARE RITUAL COULD YOU ADD INTO YOUR DAY TO BRING MORE PEACE?

....
....
....

🏆 WINS FOR THE DAY

TODAY I ACCOMPLISHED . . .

....
....
....
....

☁ MY THOUGHTS & NOTES

....
....
....
....
....

Your vulnerability is a gift to yourself, because it allows you to feel alive.

I FEEL . . . 😃 😍 😐 😴 🙁 😣   I WANT TO FEEL ....

🫶 GRATITUDE CHECK

TODAY I AM GRATEFUL FOR . . .

1. ....
2. ....
3. ....

THINK ABOUT THINGS
YOU SEE IN THE WORLD
THAT ARE RIGHT AND JUST.
THROUGHOUT THE DAY,
MAKE A POINT OF FINDING
MORE THINGS
TO APPRECIATE ABOUT
THE WORLD.

💡 DAILY AFFIRMATIONS

1. ....
2. ....
3. ....

BONUS: *Read each affirmation 10x in the mirror & throughout the day for faster results.*

☀ 3 PRIORITY GOALS

1. ....
2. ....
3. ....

💭 MY THOUGHTS & NOTES

Self-Care Check

○ **PHYSICAL**
Move or rest.

○ **SOCIAL**
Quality conversation.

○ **SPIRITUAL**
Good for the soul.

○ **HOUSEHOLD**
Cleaning or organizing.

○ **PAMPERING**
Treat yourself.

○ **PERSONAL**
Time on a hobby.

○ **EMOTIONAL**
Honor feelings.

○ **MENTAL**
Read or learn.

Be happy because of the hope you have. Be patient when you have troubles. Pray all the time. —Romans 12:12

♡ GRATITUDE CHECK

TONIGHT I AM GRATEFUL FOR . . .

1. ....
2. ....
3. ....

Wellness Check

○ WORKOUT ○ NATURE

○ MEDITATION CAFFEINE: ....

○ NUTRITION STEPS: ....

WATER INTAKE:

🧠 MENTAL HEALTH CHECK

RIGHT NOW I FEEL . . . (YOU MAY CHOOSE MORE THAN ONE)

○ HAPPY	○ PEACEFUL	○ PROUD
○ LOVING	○ CREATIVE	○ SAD
○ HOPEFUL	○ STRESSED	○ TIRED
○ CALM	○ ANNOYED	○ SCARED
○ ANGRY	○ POSITIVE	○ JOYFUL
○ OVERWHELMED	○ ANXIOUS	○ ....

WHAT IS YOUR DREAM VACATION?

....
....
....

🏆 WINS FOR THE DAY

TODAY I ACCOMPLISHED . . .

....
....
....
....

☁ MY THOUGHTS & NOTES

....
....
....
....
....

I don't smile because life is perfect. I smile because no matter what, I'm going to choose to be happy in this moment.

@POSITIVEKRISTEN

HAVE I FELT A BOOST OF HAPPINESS LATELY? ✓ ✗

WHAT HAVE I LEARNED IN THE PAST 30 DAYS?

....
....
....
....

WHAT NEW HABITS HAVE I ACQUIRED?

....
....
....
....

WHAT CHALLENGES HAVE I HAD TO WORK ON?

....
....
....
....

WHAT ARE MY NEXT STEPS?

....
....
....
....

Thoughts & Notes

Thoughts & Notes

Thoughts & Notes

Thoughts & Notes

Thoughts & Notes

Thoughts & Notes

Thoughts & Notes

Endnotes

1. Ulrich Orth and Richard W. Robins, "Is High Self-Esteem Beneficial? Revisiting a Classic Question," *American Psychologist* 77, no. 1 (January 2022): pp. 5-17, https://doi.org/10.1037/amp0000922

2. "You Can Change Your DNA," HeartMath Institute, June 15, 2015, https://www.heartmath.org/articles-of-the-heart/personal-development/you-can-change-your-dna/.

3. Karuna Meda, "How to Manipulate Brain Waves for a Better Mental State," *The Nexus*, November 26, 2019, https://nexus.jefferson.edu/science-and-technology/how-to-manipulate-brain-waves-for-a-better-mental-state/.

4. Tara Well, "Compassion at the Mirror," *Psychology Today* (Sussex Publishers, March 24, 2019), https://www.psychologytoday.com/us/blog/the-clarity/201903/compassion-the-mirror.

5. Marie Forleo, "Self-Made Millionaire: The Simple Strategy That Helped Increase My Odds of Success by 42%," CNBC, September 13, 2019, https://www.cnbc.com/2019/09/13/self-made-millionaire-how-to-increase-your-odds-of-success-by-42-percent-marie-forleo.html.

6. Meda, "How to Manipulate Brain Waves for a Better Mental State."

Acknowledgments

This journal is dedicated to the Power of Positivity community. Thank you for believing in my work and this movement. I am so grateful and inspired by your commitment to improve your life and make the world a better place.

Special thanks to the readers who have my first journal, the *3 Minute Positivity Journal*. Without your support and incredibly positive feedback, I'm not sure if I would have created this second journal. Your feedback motivated me to create a new journal and make this journal even more impactful.

Extra special thanks to those who not only started the first journal, but completed it and continued the habit with another one. I am blown away by the number of people who have written to me about how their life has completely changed. Shout-out to Jeanne Mutziger, who has completed four journals—unbelievable. You are amazing and inspire us all!

I also want to give special acknowledgment to the team at Hay House—I am grateful for everyone who helped me along the way. Thank you for believing in me and my mission to uplift the planet. Special shout-out to Patty Gift (you are literally such a gift) for partnering with me to distribute these journals globally and in stores. Special thanks to my editor, Anne Barthel, for always making the process fun, enjoyable, and impactful. What beautiful teamwork!

Thank you to my PoP team, especially Ellie Shoja, Stephanie Wallace, Rupa Limbu, and David Papanikolau. I am beyond blessed to work with such incredible souls who are so passionate about what they do.

Last, but certainly not least, this journal is dedicated to YOU. I am grateful for your support. Whether we have been connected for a long time or now through this journal, thank you! As you read the pages of this book and begin taking action daily, may it be a stepping stone toward living your fullest, most joyful expression of who you really are. Thank you for being on this journey with me. Now, let's stay connected!

About the Author

Kristen Butler's mission is to uplift the planet! She is the CEO and founder of Power of Positivity and the best-selling author of the *3 Minute Positivity Journal*. She started PoP in 2009 after hitting rock bottom and bouncing back using the power of positivity.

Kristen has a background in social media and journalism since 1998. She is passionate about helping others boost their mood, train their brain, and improve their life. Passionate about nature, Kristen lives in the heart of the Blue Ridge Mountains in North Carolina with her husband, daughters, and furbabies. Her interests and hobbies include hiking, studying, writing, health and fitness, traveling, and plant-based nutrition.

Kristen has dramatically transformed her life in *many* areas and has a strong desire to help others. Connect with her online and on social media:

⊕ positivekristen.com

❙ facebook.com/positivekristen

▣ instagram.com/positivekristen

🐦 twitter.com/positivekristen